FROM PONKAPOG TO PESTH.

THOMAS BAILEY ALDRICH

FROM

PONKAPOG TO PESTH

BOSTON
HOUGHTON, MIFFLIN AND COMPANY
New York: 11 East Seventeenth Street
The Riverside Press, Cambridge
1883

The Riverside Press, Cambridge:
Electrotyped and Printed by H. O. Houghton & Co.

CONTENTS.

As for thefe Obferuations which I now exhibite vnto thy gentle cenfure, take them I pray thee in good part till I prefent better vnto thee after my next trauels.

CORYAT'S CRUDITIES. 1611.

I.
PROLOGUE.

FROM PONKAPOG TO PESTH.

I.

PROLOGUE.

THE reader will probably not find Ponk-apog set down in any but the very latest gazetteer. It is the Indian name of a little New England village, from which the wri-ter sallied forth, a while ago, on a pilgrim-age beyond the sea. Ponkapog scarcely merits a description, and Pesth —the far-thest point east to which his wanderings led him — has been too often described. He is thus happily relieved of the onus of making strictly good the title of these papers, whose chief merit, indeed, is that they treat of neither Pesth nor Ponkapog.

It was a roundabout road the writer took to reach the Hungarian capital — a road that carried him as far north as Inverness, as far south as Naples, and left him free to saunter leisurely through Spain and spend a day in Africa. But the ground he passed over had been worn smooth by the feet of millions of tourists and paved three deep with books of travel. He was too wise to let anything creep into his note-book beyond a strip of landscape here and there, a street scene in sepia, or an outline sketch of some custom or peculiarity that chanced to strike his fancy — and these he offers modestly to the reader.

What is newest to one in foreign countries is not always the people, but their surroundings, and those same little details of life and circumstance which make no impression on a man in his own land until he returns to it after a prolonged absence, and then they stand out very sharply for a while. Neither an Italian, nor a Frenchman, nor a Saxon is worth travelling three thousand miles by sea to look upon. It is

Naples, and not the Neapolitan, that lingers in your memory. If your memory accepts the Neapolitan, it is always with a bit of Renaissance architecture adhering to him, with a stretch of background that shall include his pathetic donkey, the blue bay, the sullen peak of Vesuvius, and gray Capri in the distance. If you could transport the man bodily to New York, the only thing left to do would be to drop him into the Hudson. He would be like Emerson's sparrow, that no longer pleased when he was removed from the context of sky and river. It is the details that attract or repel more than we are aware. How sensitive to details is the eye, unconsciously taking their stamp on its retina and retaining the impression forever! It is many a day since the writer was in the old walled town of Chester; he does not recall a single feature of the hundreds of men and women he met in those quiet, gable-shadowed streets; but on the door of a house there, in a narrow court, was a grotesque bronze knocker which caught his eye for an instant in passing: that knocker somehow screwed itself to his mind without his cognizance, and now at intervals, even after all these nights and days, it raps very distinctly on his memory.

II.

DAYS WITH THE DEAD.

II.

DAYS WITH THE DEAD.

I.

THEY have a fashion across the water, particularly on the Continent, of making much of their dead. A fifteenth or a sixteenth century celebrity is a revenue to the church or town in which the distinguished ashes may chance to repose. It would be an interesting operation, if it were practicable, to draw a line between the local reverence for the virtues of the deceased and that strictly mundane spirit which regards him as assets. The two are so nicely dovetailed that I fancy it would be quite impossible, in most instances, to say where the one ends and the other begins.

In the case of the good Cardinal Borromeo, for example. The good cardinal died

in 1584.   He is one of the loveliest figures
in history.   Nobly born, rich, and learned,
he devoted himself and his riches to holy
deeds.   The story of his life is a record of
beautiful sacrifices and unselfish charities.
Though his revenue was princely, his quick
sympathies often left him as destitute as
a Franciscan friar.   His vast possessions
finally dwindled to a meagre patrimony.
During the great plague at Milan, in 1576,
he sold what was left of his plate and furniture to buy bread for the famishing people.   When he died, all Italy wept for
him like one pair of eyes.   He lies in the
crypt of the cathedral at Milan.   It is
dark down in the crypt; but above him
are carvings and gildings and paintings,
basking in the mellow light sifted through
the immense choir windows —

> "Innumerable of stains and splendid dyes
> As are the tiger-moth's deep-damasked wings."

Above the fretted roof the countless "stat-
ued pinnacles" lift themselves into the blue

air. How magical all that delicate needle-work of architecture looks, by moonlight or sunlight!

> "O Milan, O the chanting quires,
>   The giant windows' blazoned fires,
>   The height, the space, the gloom, the glory!
>   A mount of marble, a hundred spires!"

When they show you the embalmed body of Borromeo — for it is really the body and not merely the sarcophagus they show you — the *custode*, a priest, lights the high candles on either side of the silver-encrusted altar. The cardinal's remains are kept in an hermetically-sealed case of rock crystal set within a massive oak coffin, one side of which is lowered by a windlass. There he lies in his jeweled robes, with his gloved hands crossed on his bosom and his costly crosier at his side, just as they laid him away in 1584. The features are wonderfully preserved, and have not lost the placid expression they wore when he fell asleep, — that look of dreamy serenity

2

peculiar to the faces of dead persons. The head is bald, and as black as ebony. There were services going on, the day we visited the cathedral. Above us the crowds came and went on the mosaic pavements, but no sound of the outside world penetrated to the dim, begemmed chapel where Carlo Borromeo, count, cardinal, and saint, takes what rest he can. We stood silent in the unflaring candlelight, gazing on the figure which had been so beloved in Milan three centuries ago. Presently the black-robed *custode* turned the noiseless crank, and the coffin side slowly ascended to its place. It was all very solemn and impressive — too impressive and too solemn altogether for so small a sum as five francs.

I am but an intermittent worshiper of saints; yet I have an ineradicable belief in good men like Carlo Borromeo, and, as he has long since finished his earthly tasks, I think it would be showing the cardinal greater respect to bury him than to exhibit him. He nearly spoiled my visit to Milan. I resolved to have no further commerce with the dead, directly or indirectly. But the dead play a very prominent part in the experience of the wanderer abroad. The houses in which they were born, the tombs in which they lie, the localities they made famous by their good or evil deeds, and the works their genius left behind them are necessarily the chief shrines of his pilgrimage. You leave London with a distincter memory of the monuments in Westminster Abbey and St. Paul's than of the turbulent streams of life that surge through the Strand. Mr. Blank, to whom you bore a letter of introduction, is not so real a person to you as John Milton, whose grave you saw at St. Giles's, Cripplegate or De Foe, who sleeps in the melancholy Bunhill Fields Burial Ground. You catch yourself assisting, with strange relish, at the burning of heretics at Smithfield. Ridley and Latimer stand before you in flesh and bone

and flame at Oxford. Thomas à Becket
falls stabbed at your feet on the stone flagging in Canterbury Cathedral. At Holy-
rood, are not Darnley and pallid Ruthven
in his steel corselet forever creeping up
that narrow spiral staircase leading to the
small cabinet where Rizzio is supping with
the luckless queen? You cannot escape
these things if you would. Your railway
carriage takes you up at one famous grave
and sets you down at another. Madrid is
but a stepping-stone to the gloomy Escorial,
with its underground library of gilded coffins — a library of royal octavos, one might
say, for none but Spanish kings and queens
are shelved there.[1] In Paris, where the
very atmosphere thrills with intense life,

[1] Spanish post-mortem etiquette excludes the late Queen
Mercedes from this apartment, as none but queens who have
been mothers of kings are allowed sanctuary here. On a
shelf at the left of the entrance to the tomb, an empty sarcophagus, of the same ornate pattern as the others, awaits
Alfonso III. It would probably not wait long for him if
Spanish republicanism had its will.

you are brought at each step face to face
with the dead. What people are these
that flit in groups up and down the brilliant boulevards? *They* are not sipping
absinthe and taking their ease — the poor
ghosts, old and new! Can you stand in
the Place de la Concorde and not think
of the twenty-eight hundred persons who
were guillotined there between 1793 and
1795? A few minutes' walk from the
crowded *cafés* leads you to the morgue,
"the little Doric morgue," as Browning
calls it. The golden dome of the Invalides
keeps perpetually in your mind "the ter-
ror of Europe," held down by sixty tons
of porphyry, in the rotunda. The neatly-
swept asphalt under your feet ran blood
but yesterday. Here it was, near the Tui-
leries, the insurgents threw up a barricade.
Those white spots which you observe on
the façade of yonder building, the Made-
leine, are bits of new stone set into the
sacrilegious shot-holes. On the verge of

the city, and within sound of its feverish
heart-throb, stretch Père la Chaise and
Montmartre and Mont Parnasse, pathetic
with renowned names.

I suppose that a taste for churchyards
and cemeteries is a cultivated taste. At
home they were entirely disconnected in
my mind with any thought of enjoyment;
but after a month on the other side I pre-
ferred a metropolitan graveyard to almost
any object of interest that could be presented to me. A cemetery at home sug-
gests awkward possibilities; but nothing of
the kind occurs to you in rambling through
a foreign burial-ground. As our *gamins*
would say, it is not your funeral. You
wander along the serpentine walk as you
would stroll through a picture gallery.
You as little think of adding a mound to
the one as you would of contributing a
painting to the other. You survey the
monoliths and the bas-reliefs and the urns
and the miniature Athenian temples from

the stand-point of an unbiased spectator who has paid his admittance fee and expects entertainment or instruction. Some of the pleasantest hours I passed in sight-seeing were spent in graveyards. Among the most notable things we saw were the Jewish cemetery at Prague, with its smoky Gothic synagogue of the thirteenth century (the *Altneuschule*), and the ancient churchyard of St. John at Nuremberg, where Hans Sachs and many another worthy of his day lie at rest, and where the remains of Albrecht Dürer once rested — painter, poet, architect, and engraver, the master of almost everything except Mrs. Dürer. The engraved brass plates — the P. P. C. cards, so to speak, of the departed aristocracy of Nuremberg — on the horizontal slabs of St. John's are very quaint, with their crests, and coats-of-arms, and symbols of gentility. At Prague the stones are marked with pitchers and hands, to designate the descendants of the tribes of

Levi and Aaron. They claim to have one stone that dates as far back as A. D. 606. Some of the graves are held in great veneration; that of Rabbi Abignor Kara, who died in 1439, is often made the point of pilgrimage by Jews living in distant lands. Within the yard is a building where the funeral rites are performed, and grave-clothes are kept for all comers. The dead millionaire and the dead pauper are arrayed in the same humble garb, and alike given to earth in a rough board coffin. The Jewish custom, like death itself, is no respecter of persons. There is a fine austerity in this.

II.

It was always more or less of a satisfaction to observe that the mortuary sculptures of the Old World were every whit as hideous as our own. The sepulchral designs in churches abroad are generally in the worst style of Middle Age realism. A half-draped skeleton of Death, plunging his dart into the bosom of some emaciated marble girl, seems to have been a consoling symbol to the survivors a few centuries ago. This ghastly fancy is constantly under your eyes. If I call it ghastly I give expression to the effect it produced on me at first. It would not be honest for me to affirm that I did not like it at last. I became so accustomed to this skeleton and his brother monstrosities that when we visited those three grim chambers under the Church of the Capuchins at Rome,

and saw the carefully polished skulls of
hundreds of monks wrought into pillars
and arches and set upon shelves, I looked
at them as complacently as if they had
been a lot of exploded percussion-caps.
"It is a pity they can't be used again,"
I thought; and that was all. I began to
believe the beautiful economy of nature
to be greatly overrated.

This is the burial-place of the Cappuc-
cini, who esteem it a blissful privilege to
lie here for a few years in consecrated
earth brought from Jerusalem, and then,
when their graves are wanted for fresher
brothers, to be taken up and transformed
into architectural decorations. The walls
and recesses and arched ceilings of these
chapels (which are beneath the church
but not under ground) are thus orna-
mented with the brotherhood skillfully arranged in fanciful devices, the finger-joints
and the fragile links of the vertebral column being wrought into friezes and light

cornices, and the larger bones arranged in diamonds and hearts and rounds, like the sabres and bayonets in an armory. Here and there on the ceiling is a complete skeleton set into the plaster, quite suggestive of a cool outline by Flaxman or Retzsch. The poor monks! they were not very ornamental in life; but time is full of compensations. Death seems to have relieved them of one unhappy characteristic. " There is no disagreeable scent," says the author of The Marble Faun, describing this place, " such as might have been expected from the decay of so many holy persons, in whatever odor of sanctity they may have taken their departure. The same number of living monks would not smell half so unexceptionably." The Capuchin golgotha is more striking than the Roman or the Parisian catacombs, for the reason that its contracted limits do not allow you to escape from the least of its horrible grotesqueness. In the catacombs you are impressed by their extent rather than by anything else.

Rome is one enormous mausoleum. There the Past lies visibly stretched upon his bier. There is no to-day or to-morrow in Rome ; it is perpetual yesterday. One might lift up a handful of dust anywhere and say, with the Persian poet, " This was once man." Where everything has been so long dead, a death of to-day seems almost an impertinence. How quickly and with what serene irony the new grave is absorbed by the universal antiquity of the place ! The block of marble over Keats does not appear a day fresher than the neighboring Pyramid of Caius Cestius. Oddly enough, we saw no funeral in Rome. In almost every other large city it was our fate, either as we entered or departed, to meet a funeral cortege. Every one stands uncovered as the train crawls by, the vehicles come to a halt at the curbstone, the children stop their play, heads are bowed, golden locks and gray, on every side. As I have said, though in a different sense, they make much of their dead abroad. I was struck by the contrast the day we reached home. Driving from the steamer, we encountered a hearse straggling down Broadway. It attracted as much reverential regard as would be paid to an ice-cart.

I happened to witness a picturesque funeral in Venice. It was that of a chorus-boy, in a church on one of the smaller canals somewhere west of the Rialto. I stumbled on the church accidentally that forenoon, and was not able to find it again the next day — a circumstance to which the incident perhaps owes the illusory atmosphere that envelops it for me. The building had disappeared, like Aladdin's palace, in the night.

They were performing a mass as I entered. The great rose window behind the organ and the chancel windows were darkened with draperies, and the colossal candles

were burning. The coffin, covered with a
heavily embroidered pall, stood on an elevated platform in front of the magnificent
altar. The inlaid columns glistening in the
candle-light, the smoke of the incense curl-
ing lazily up past the baldachino to the
frescoed dome, the priests in elaborate stoles
and chasubles kneeling around the bier —
it was like a masterly composed picture.
When the ceremonies were concluded, the
coffin was lifted from the platform by six
young friars and borne to a gondola in
waiting at the steps near the portals. The
priests, carrying a huge golden crucifix
and several tall gilt torches, unlighted,
crowded into the bow and stern of the
floating hearse, which was attached by a
long rope to another gondola occupied by
oarsmen. Following these were two or
three covered gondolas whose connection
with the obsequies was not clear to me, as
they appeared to be empty. Slowly down
the narrow canal, in that dead stillness

which reigns in Venice, swept the sombre flotilla, bearing its unconscious burden to the Campo Santo. The air was full of vagrant spring scents, and the sky that arched over all was carved of one vast, unclouded sapphire. In the deserted church were two old crones scraping up the drippings of the wax candles from the tessellated pavement. Nothing except time is wasted in Italy.

I saw a more picturesque though not so agreeable a funeral in Florence. The night of our arrival was one of those unearthly moonlight nights which belong to Italy. The Arno, changed to a stream of quicksilver, flowed swiftly through the stone arches of the Ponte Vecchio under our windows, and lured me with its beauty out-of-doors, though a great clock somewhere near by had just clanged eleven. By an engraving I had seen in boyhood I recognized the bridge of Taddeo Gaddi, with its goldsmith shops on either side. They were closed now, of course. I strolled across

the bridge and back again, once or twice,
and then wandered off into a network of
dingy streets, traversed by one street so
very narrow that you saw only a hand's
breadth of amethystine sky between the
tops of the tall buildings. Standing in the
middle of the thoroughfare, I could almost touch the shutters of the shops right
and left. At the upper end of the street,
which was at least three quarters of a
mile in length, the overhanging fronts of
the lofty houses seemed to meet and shut
out the dense moonlight. In the desperate struggle which took place there between the moon and the gloom, a hundred fantastic shadows slipped from coigne
and cornice and fell into the street below,
like besiegers flung from the ramparts of
some old castle. Not a human being nor a
light was anywhere visible. Suddenly I
saw what, for an instant, I took to be a
falling star in the extreme distance. It
approached in a zigzag course. It broke

into several stars ; these grew larger ; then I discovered they were torches. A low monotonous chant, like the distant chorus of demons in an opera, reached my ear. The chant momently increased in distinctness, and as the torches drew nearer I saw that they were carried by fifteen or twenty persons marching in a square, in the middle of which was a bier supported by a number of ghostly figures. The procession was sweeping down on me at the rate of six miles an hour ; the training pall flapped in the wind caused by the velocity of the march. When the cortége was within twenty or thirty yards of me, I noticed that the trestle-bearers and the persons who held the flambeaux were shrouded from forehead to foot in white sheets with holes pierced for the eyes. I never beheld anything more devilish. On they came, occupying the whole width of the narrow street. I had barely time to crowd myself into a projecting doorway, when they swept by with a rhyth-

3

mical swinging gait, to the measure of their awful threnody. I waited until the muffled chant melted into the distance — and then I made a bee-line for the hotel.

In Italy the hour of interment is graduated by the worldly position of the deceased. The poor are buried in the daytime ; thus the expense of torches is avoided. Illuminated night-funerals are reserved for the wealthy and persons of rank. At least, I believe that such is the regulation, though the reverse of this order may be the case. At Naples, I know, the interments in the Campo Santo Vecchio take place a little before sunset. Shelley said of the Protestant Burying Ground at Rome that the spot was lovely enough to make one in love with death. Nobody would dream of saying that about the Campo Santo at Naples — a parallelogram of several hundred feet in length, inclosed on three sides by a high wall and on the fourth by an arcade. In this dreary space, approached through a dismal avenue of cypresses, are three hundred and sixty-six deep pits, one of which is opened each evening to receive the dead of that day, and then sealed up — one pit for each day of the year. I conjecture that the extra pit must be for leap-year. Only the poorest persons, paupers and waifs, are buried here, if it can be called buried. The body is usually left unattended at the arcade, to await its turn.

There is a curious burial custom at Munich. The law requires that every man, woman, and child who dies within city limits shall lie in state for three days in the Leichenhaus (dead house) of the Gottesacker, the southern cemetery, outside the Sendling Gate. This is to prevent any chance of premature burial, an instance of which, many years ago, gave rise to the present provision. The Leichenhaus is comprised of three large chambers or *salons*, in which the dead are placed upon raised couches and surrounded by flowers. A series of wide windows giving upon the arcade affords the public an unobstructed view of the interior. The spectacle is not so repellant as one might anticipate. The neatly-kept, well-lighted rooms, the profusion of flowers, and the scrupulous propriety which prevails in all the arrangements make the thing as little terrible as possible. On the Sunday of our visit to the Gottesacker, the place was unusually full of bodies awaiting interment — old men and women, young girls and infants. Some were like exquisite statues, others like wax-figures, and all piteous. Attached to the hand of each adult was a string or wire connected with a bell in the custodian's apartment. It would be difficult to imagine a more startling sound than would be the sudden kling-kling of one of those same bells!

But I have been playing too long what Balzac calls a *solo de corbillard.*

III.

BEGGARS, PROFESSIONAL AND AMATEUR.

III.

BEGGARS, PROFESSIONAL AND AMATEUR.

THERE is one thing that sometimes comes near taking the joy out of the heart of foreign travel. It is one of those trifles which frequently prove a severer test to philosophy than calamities. In the East this thing is called *bakhshîsh*, in Germany *trinkgeld*, in Italy *buonamano*, in France *pourboire*, in England — I do not know how it is called in England, but it is called for pretty often. In whatever soft, insidious syllable it may wrap itself, it is nothing but hateful. A piece of money which is not earned by honest service, but is extracted from you as a matter of course by any vagabond who may start out of the bowels of the earth, like a gnome or a kobold, at the sound of your footfall, is a shameless coin: it debases him that gives and him that takes.

Everywhere on the Continent the tourist is looked upon as a bird to be plucked, and presently the bird himself feebly comes to regard plucking as his proper destiny, and abjectly holds out his wing so long as there is a feather left on it. I say everywhere on the Continent; but, indeed, a man of ordinary agility might walk over the greater part of Europe on outstretched palms. Russians and Americans have the costly reputation of being lavish of money on their travels — the latter are pictured by the fervid Italian imagination as residing in gold-mines located in California and various parts of the State of New York — and are consequently favorites. The Frenchman is too artful and the Briton too brusque to cut up well as victims. The Italian rarely ventures far from his accustomed flea, but when he does, like the German (who, on the other hand, is fond of travel-

ling), he voyages on a most economical
basis. He carries off the unburnt candle-
end, and his gratuities are homœopathic.
In spite of his cunning, I have no doubt —
I should be sorry to doubt — that his own
countrymen skin him alive. It is gratify-
ing to be assured by Mr. Howells, in his
Italian Journeys, that "these ingenious
people prey upon their own kind with an
avidity as keen as that with which they
devour strangers;" he is even "half per-
suaded that a ready-witted foreigner fares
better among them than a traveller of their
own nation." Nevertheless, I still think
that the privilege of being an American is
one of the most costly things in Europe.
It is ever a large, though invisible, item in
your account, whether you halt at a Parisian hôtel or a snuffy *posada* in Catalo-
nia. In neither place has the landlord the
same excuse for extortion that was offered
by the Ostend inn-keeper to the major-
domo of George II., on one of his trips

from England to Hanover. "Are eggs scarce in Ostend?" inquired the major-domo, with supercilious eyebrows. "No," returned the honest landlord, "but kings are." Americans are not scarce anywhere.

In Italy one is besieged by beggars, morning, noon, and night; a small coin generally suffices, and a modicum of good nature always goes a great way. There is something innocent in their deepest strategy, and something very winning in the amiability with which they accept the situation when their villainy is frustrated. Sometimes, however, when the petitioner is not satisfied with your largess — as always happens when you give him more than he expects — he is scarcely polite. I learned this from a venerable ex-sailor in Genoa. "Go, brigand!" was the candid advice of that ancient mariner. He then fell to cursing my relatives, the family tomb, and everything appertaining to me — with my coin warming in his pocket.

It is fair to observe that the Italian beggar usually renders tribute to an abstract idea of manhood by assuming that he has done you some sort of service. This service is not generally visible to the unaided eye, and I fancy that the magnifying glass of sufficient power to enable you always to detect it has yet to be invented. But it is to his everlasting praise that he often does try to throw a veil of decency over the naked injustice of his demand, though he is too apt to be content with the thinnest of fabrics. I have paid a Neapolitan gentleman ten sous for leaning against a deadwall in front of a hotel window. The unexpectedness and the insinuating audacity of the appeals frequently take away your presence of mind, and leave you limp. There was an old son of Naples who dwelt on a curb-stone near the Castell dell' Ovo. Stumbling on his private public residence quite unintentionally, one forenoon, I was immediately assessed. Ever after he claimed me, and finally brought his son-in-law to me, and introduced him as a person combining many of the most desirable qualities of a pensioner. One of his strong points was that he had been accidentally carried off to America, having fallen asleep one day in the hold of a fruit vessel.

"But, sir," I said, "why should I give you anything? I don't know you."

"That is the reason, signor."

At bottom it was an excellent reason. If I paid the father-in-law for the pleasure of knowing him, was it not logical and just that I should pay the son-in-law for the much greater pleasure I had had in not knowing him? The slightest thing will serve, in Italy, for a lien upon your exchequer. An urchin who turns himself into a Catherine-wheel at your carriage side, or stands on his head under the very hoofs of your horses, approaches you with the confidence of a prodigal son. A three-day-old nosegay thrown into your lap gives a small

Italian maiden in one garment the right to
cling to the footboard of your *vettura* until
you reimburse her. In driving from Pompeii to Sorrento, no fewer than fifty of
these floral tributes will be showered upon
you. The little witches who throw the
flowers are very often pretty enough to be
caught and sculptured. An inadvertent
glance towards a fellow sleeping by the
roadside places you at once in a false position. I have known an even less compro-
mising thing than a turn of the eyelid to
establish financial relations between the
stranger and the native. I have known a
sneeze to do it. One morning, on the Mole
at Venice, an unassuming effort of my own
in this line was attended by a most unexpected result. Eight or ten young raga-
muffins, who had been sunning themselves
at a gondola-landing, instantly started up
from a recumbent posture and advanced
upon me in a semicircle, with "*Salute,
signor, salute!*" One of these youths dis-

turbed a preconceived impression of mine
by suddenly exclaiming, —

"I am a boy Americano, dam!"

As I had not come so far from home to
relieve the necessities of my own countrymen, and as I reflected that possibly this
rogue's companions were also profane Americani, I gave them nothing but a genial
smile, which they divided among them with
the resignation that seems to be a national trait.

The transatlantic impostor, like Meph-
istopheles, has as many shapes as men have
fancies. Sometimes he keeps a shop, and
sometimes he turns a hand-organ. Now he
looks out at you from the cowl of a mediæval monk, and now you behold him in a
white choker, pretending to be a verger.
You become at last so habituated to seeing
persons approach *in formâ pauperis*, that
your barber seems to lack originality when
he "leaves it to your generosity," though
he has a regular tariff for his local patrons.

He does not dare name a price in your case, though the price were four or five times above his usual rate, for he knows that you would unhesitatingly accept his terms, and his existence would be forever blighted by the reflection that he might have charged you more.

These things, I repeat, cease to amaze one after a while, though I plead guilty to a new sensation the day a respectable Viennese physician left it to my generosity. I attempted to reason with Herr Doctor Scheister, but quite futilely. No, it was so he treated princes and Americans. It was painful to see a member of a noble profession, not to say the noblest, placing himself on a level with grooms and barbers and venders of orange-wood walking-sticks. But the intelligent Herr Doctor Scheister was content to do that.

In many cities the street beggar is under the strict surveillance of the police; yet there is no spot in Europe but has its

empty palm. It is only in Italy, however,
that pauperism is a regular branch of industry. There it has been elevated to a
fine art. Elsewhere it is a sordid, clumsy
make-shift, with no joy in it. It falls
short of being a gay science in France or
Germany, or Austria or Hungary. In Scot-
land it is depressing, in Spain humiliating.
In Spain the beggar is loftily condescend-
ing; he is a *caballero*, a man of *sangre azul*,
and has his coat-of-arms, though he may
have no arms to his coat, *caramba!* In
order to shake him off you are obliged to
concede his quality. He will never leave
you until his demand is complied with, or
until you say, "Brother, for the love of
God, excuse me!" and then the rogue departs with a careless "God go with you!"
He is precisely the person whom you would
not be anxious to meet in a deserted *calle*
after nightfall, or by daylight in a pass of
the Guadarrama. The guide-books give
disheartening accounts of mendicancy in

Ireland ; but that must be in the interior. I saw nothing of it along the coast, at Dublin and Cork. I encountered only one beggar in Ireland, at Queenstown, who retired crest-fallen when I informed him in English that I was a Frenchman and did n't understand him.

"Thrue for ye," he said ; "bad 'cess to me, what was I thinkin' ov ! "

On the rising and falling inflection of that brogue I returned to America quite independently of a Cunard steamer. I had to call the man back and pay my passage.

In England you are subjected to a different kind of extortion. There are beggars enough and to spare in the larger cities ; but that is not the class which preys upon you in Merrie England. It is the middle-aged housekeeper, the smart chambermaid, the elegiac waiter and his assistant, the boy in buttons who opens the hall door, the frowzy subterranean person called

4

Boots, the coachman, the ostler, and one or two other individuals whose precise relevancy to your affairs will always remain a pleasing mystery to you, but who nevertheless stand in a line with the rest in the hall of the wayside inn, at your departure, and expect a gratuity. They each look for a fee ranging from two to ten shillings sterling, according to the length of your sojourn, though a very magnificent charge for attendance has already been recorded in your bill, which appears to have been drawn up by an amateur mathematician of somewhat uncertain touch as yet in the intricate art of addition.

The English cousin of the American workingman, who would feel inclined to knock you down if you offered him money for telling you the time of day, will very placidly pocket a fee for that heavy service. In walking the streets of London you never get over your astonishment at that eminently respectable person in black —

your conjecture makes him a small curate or a tutor in some institution of learning — who, after answering your trivial question, takes the breath out of you by suggesting his willingness to drink your 'ealth.

On the whole, I am not certain that I do not prefer the graceful, foliage-like, vagabond ways of Pietro and Giuliana to the icy mendicity of Jeemes.

IV.

WAYS AND MANNERS.

IV.

WAYS AND MANNERS.

I ONCE asked an American friend, who had spent half his life in foreign travel, to tell me what one thing most impressed him in his various wanderings. I supposed that he was going to say the Pyramids or the Kremlin at Moscow. His reply was, " The politeness and consideration I have met with from every one except travelling English-men and Americans."

I was afterwards told by an impolite person that this politeness was merely a surface polish ; but it is a singularly agreeable sort of veneer. Some one says that if any of us were peeled, a savage would be found at the core. It is a very great merit, then, to have this savage wrapped in numerous folds, and rendered as hard to peel as possible. For the most part, the pilgrim abroad comes in contact with only the outside of men and things. The main point is gained if that outside is pleasant.

The American at home enjoys a hundred conveniences which he finds wanting in the heart of European civilization. Many matters which we consider as necessities here are regarded as luxuries there, or not known at all. A well-appointed private house in an American city has perfections in the way of light, heat, water, ventilation, drainage, etc., that are not to be obtained even in palaces abroad; indeed, a palace is the last place in which they are to be looked for. The traveller is constantly amused by the primitive agricultural implements which he sees employed in some parts of France, Italy, and Germany, by the ingenuous devices they have for watering the streets of their grand capitals, and by the strange disregard of economy in man-power in everything. A water-cart in Berlin, for illustration, requires three men to manage it : one

to drive, and two on foot behind to twitch
right and left, by means of ropes, a short
hose with a sprinkler at the end.

> " I wondered what they would be at
> Under the lindens."

This painful hose, attached to a chubby
Teutonic-looking barrel, has the appearance
of being the tail of some wretched nonde-
script animal, whose sufferings would in our
own land invoke the swift interposition of
the humane. That this machine is wholly
inadequate to the simple duty of sprinkling
the street is a fact not perhaps worth men-
tioning. The culinary utensils of Central
Germany are, I venture to say, of nearly
the same pattern as those used by Eve —
judging by some earthenware and iron-
mongery of which I caught a glimpse in
the kitchen of the Rothe Ross at Nuremberg. I saw in Tuscany a wheelbarrow
that must have been an infringement of
an Egyptian patent of 500 B. C. I forget in
what imperial city it was I beheld a tin

bath-tub shamelessly allowing itself to be borne from door to door and let out by the job. In several respects the United States are one or two centuries in advance of the Old World; but in that little matter of veneering I have mentioned, we are very far behind her.

The incivility which greets the American traveller at every stage in his own domains is so rare an accomplishment among foreign railway, steamboat, and hotel officials that it is possible to journey from Dan to Beersheba — certainly from Ponkapog to Pesth — without meeting a single notable instance of it. I think that the gentlemen of the Dogana at Ventimiglia were selected expressly on account of their high breeding to examine luggage at that point. In France — by France I mean Paris — even the drivers of the public carriages are civil. Civilization can go no further. If Darwin is correct in his theory of the survival of the fittest, there will

ultimately not be a single specimen of the
genus left anywhere in America. We shall
have to import Parisians. I am not positive but we shall also run short of railway
conductors and ticket-sellers. We have
persons occupying these posts here who
could not hold similar positions in Europe
fifteen minutes.

The guard who has charge of your carriage on a Continental railway, so far from
being the disdainful autocrat who on our
own cars too often snatches your ticket
from you and snubs you at a word, is the
most thoughtful and considerate of men;
he looks after the welfare and comfort of
your party as if that were the specialty for
which he was created; he never loses countenance at your daring French or German,
or the graceful New England accent you
throw upon your Italian; he is ready with
the name of that ruined castle which stands
like a jagged tooth in the mouth of the
mountain gorge; he does not neglect to tell

you at what station you may find an excellent buffet; you cannot weary him with
questions; he will smilingly answer the
same one a hundred times; and when he is
killed in a collision with the branch train,
you are not afraid to think where he will
go, with all this kindliness.

I am convinced that it is the same person, thinly disguised as the proprietor of a
hotel, who receives you at the foot of the
staircase as you step down from the omni-
bus, and is again the attentive and indefati-
gable chamberlain to your earthly comfort.
It is an old friend who has been waiting for
you these many years.   To be sure, as the
proprietor of a hotel the old friend makes
you pay roundly for all this ; but do you not
pay roundly for food and shelter in taverns on your native heath, and get no civil-
ity whatever, unless the hotel-clerk has lost
his mind ? Your Continental inn-keeper,
of whatever nationality, keeps a paternal
eye on you, and does not allow you to be

imposed upon by rapacious outsiders. If you are to be imposed upon, he attends to that trifling formality himself, and always graciously. Across three thousand miles of sea and I know not how many miles of land, I touch my hat at this moment to the landlord of that snuffy little hostelry at Wittenberg, who awoke me at midnight to excuse himself for not having waited upon us in person when we arrived by the ten o'clock train. He had had a card-party — the Herr Professor Something-splatz and a few friends — in the coffee-room, and really, etc., etc. He could n't sleep, and did n't let me, until he had made his excuses. It was downright charming in you, mine host of the Goldner Adler; I thank you for it, and I 'd thank you not to do it again.

Every American who has passed a week in rural England must have carried away, even if he did not bring with him, a fondness for our former possessions. The solid

hospitality he has received at the comfortable old inns smothered in leaves and
mosses by the roadside is sure to figure
among his pleasantest reminiscences. It lies
in his recollection with Stratford and Canterbury and Grasmere ; as he thinks of it,
it takes something of the picturesqueness
of those ivy-draped abbeys and cathedrals
which went so far to satisfy his morbid
appetite for everything that is wrinkled
and demolished in the way of architecture.
It was Shenstone who said, —

> " Whoe'er has travelled life's dull round,
>   Whate'er his stages may have been,
> May sigh to think he still has found
>   The warmest welcome at an inn."

The foreign traveller will scarcely be inclined to sigh over that. If he is, he will
have cause to sigh in many an English village and in most of the leading cities across
the Channel. I know of one party that can
think with nothing but gratitude of their
reception at the hotel ———, one raw April

night, after a stormy passage from Dover to
Calais and a cheerless railway ride thence
to Paris. Rooms had been bespoken by tel-
egraph, and when the wanderers arrived at
the Rue de Rivoli they found such exquisite
preparation for their coming as seemed to
have been made by well-known gentle
hands reaching across the Atlantic. In a
small salon adjoining the parlor assigned
to the party, the wax candles threw a soft
light over the glass and silver appointments of a table spread for their repast. A
waiter arranging a dish of fruit at the
buffet greeted them with a good evening,
as if he had been their servitor for years,
instead of now laying eyes upon them
for the first time. In the open chimney-
place of the parlor was a wood fire blazing
cheerfully on the backs of a couple of brass
griffins who did not seem to mind it. On
the mantel-piece was an antique clock,
flanked by bronze candlesticks that would
have taken your heart in a bric-à-brac shop.

The furniture, the draperies, and the hundred and one nicknacks lying around on tables and *étagères*, showed the touch of a tasteful woman's hand. It might have been a room in a château. It was as unlike as possible to those gaudy barracks — fitted up at so much per yard by a soulless upholsterer — which we call parlors in our own hotels. Beyond this were the sleeping apartments, in the centre of one of which stood the neatest of *femmes de chambre*, with the demurest of dark eyes, and the pinkest of ribbons on her cap. She held in her hand a small copper pitcher of hot water, and looked like Liotard's pretty painting of the Chocolate Girl come to life. On a toilette-table under a draped mirror was a slender vase of Bohemian glass holding two or three fresh tea-roses. What beau of the old *régime* had slipped out of his sculptured tomb to pay madam that gallantry?

Outside of the larger cities on the Con-

tinent you can get as wretched accommoda-
tions as you could desire for an enemy. In
most of the German and Italian provinces,
aside from the main routes of travel, the
inns are execrable ; but the people are invariably courteous. I hardly know how to
account for the politeness which seems to
characterize every class abroad. Possibly
it is partly explained by the military sys-
tem which in many countries requires of
each man a certain term of service; the
soldier is disciplined in the severest school
of manners ; he is taught to treat both his
superior and his inferior with deference ;
courtesy becomes second nature. Certainly
it is the rule, and not the exception, among
Continental nations. From the threshold
of a broken-down chalet in some loneliest
Alpine pass you will be saluted graciously.
You grow skeptical as to that "rude Carin-
thian boor" who, in Goldsmith's poem,

"Against the houseless stranger shuts the door."

No French, Italian, or Saxon gentleman,

so far as I have observed, enters or leaves a café of the better class without lifting his hat, especially if there are ladies present. As he hurries from the railway carriage at his station — a station at which the train halts for perhaps only a few seconds — he seldom neglects to turn on the step and salute his fellow-passengers. It is true, for the last hour or two he sat staring over the top of his journal at your wife or sister; but to be a breaker of the female heart is what they all seem to aspire to, over there. It appears to be recognized as not ill-bred to stare at a lady so long as there is anything left of her. It is in that fashion that American ladies are stared at by Frenchmen and Germans and Italians and Spaniards, who, aside from this, are very polite to our countrywomen — marvellously polite when we reflect that the generality of untravelled foreigners, beyond the Straits of Dover, regard us, down deep in their hearts, as only a superior race of barbarians.

They would miss us sadly if we were to become an extinct race. Not to mention other advantages resulting from our existence, our desire to behold their paintings and statuary and the marvels of their architecture — to which they themselves are for the most part only half alive, especially in Italy — keeps a thousand of their lovely, musty old towns from collapsing. They understand this perfectly, and do whatever lies within them to interest us; they are even so obliging as to invent tombs and historic localities for our edification, and come at last to believe in them themselves. In that same Wittenberg of which I have spoken, they will show you the house of Hamlet! and at Ferrara, a high-strung sympathetic *valet-de-place*, if properly encouraged, will throw tears into his voice as he stands with you in a small cellar where by no chance is it probable that Tasso was immured for seven years, or even seven minutes. Prigione di Tasso! I have as

genuine a prison of Tasso at Ponkapog.
Though their opinion of our intelligence is
not always as flattering as we could wish,
it shall not prevent me from saying that
these people are the most charming and
courteous people on the globe, and that I
shall forget the Madonna at Dresden, the
Venus in the Louvre, and the Alhambra
as I saw it once by moonlight, before I forget an interview I witnessed one day in
the Rue de l'École de Médecine, between
a fat, red-faced concierge and a very much
battered elderly French gentleman, whose
redingote, buttoned closely up to his chin,
threw vague but still damaging suspicions
on his supply of linen.

"Pardon, madame," said the decayed old
gentleman, lifting his threadbare silk hat
by its curled brim with indescribable grace
as he approached, "is M. . . . within?"

"I think not, but I will see."

"I am pained" (*Je suis désolé*) "to give
you the trouble."

"It is no trouble, monsieur."

"Merci, madame."

The concierge disappeared. Presently she returned, loaded to the muzzle with the information that M. . . . was unfortunately not at home.

" A thousand pardons, madame, but will you have the amiability to give him this " (presenting a card that had seen better days) " as soon as he returns ? "

"Certainly, monsieur."

"Madame, I am sensible of your kindness."

"Do not speak of it."

"Bonjour, madame."

"Bonjour, monsieur."

This poor gentleman's costume was very far on its way to a paper-mill; but adversity had left his manners intact, and they were fit for palaces.

V.

A VISIT TO A CERTAIN OLD GENTLEMAN.

V.

A VISIT TO A CERTAIN OLD GENTLEMAN.

I.

It was only after the gravest consideration that we decided to visit a Certain Old Gentleman. There were so many points to be considered. It was by no means certain that a Certain Old Gentleman wanted us to visit him. Though we knew him, in a vague way, to be sure — through friends of ours who were friends of his — he did not know us at all. Then he was, according to report, a very particular old gentleman, standing squarely on his dignity, and so hedged about by conventional ideas of social etiquette, so difficult of approach, and so nearly impossible to become acquainted with when approached, that it was an audacious thing seriously to contemplate drop-

ping in on him familiarly. What impelled
us to wish to do so? Certainly we had no
desire to pay court to him. He had formerly occupied a high official position, but
now he was retired, in a manner, into private life — a sufficient reason in itself why
he should be let alone. In brief, there
were a hundred reasons why we should not
visit him, and there was not one why we
should. It was that that decided us, I
think.

It comes back to me like the reminiscence of a dream, rather than as the memory of an actual experience, that May afternoon when the purpose first unfolded itself
to us. We were sitting in the fading glow
of the day on the last of the four marble
steps which linked our parlor to the fairy-
like garden of the Albergo di Russia in
the Via Babuino. Our rooms were on the
ground-floor, and this garden, shut in on
three sides by the main building and the
wings of the hotel, and closed at the rear

by the Pincian Hill, up which the garden clambered half-way in three or four luxuriant terraces, seemed naturally to belong to our suite of apartments. All night we could hear the drip of the fountain among the cactus leaves, and catch at intervals the fragrance of orange-blooms, blown in at the one window we dared leave open. It was here we took the morning air a few minutes before breakfast; it was on these steps we smoked our cigar after the wonders of the day were done. We had the garden quite to ourselves, for the cautious tourist had long since taken wing from Rome, frightened by the early advance of summer. The great caravansary was nearly empty. Aside from the lizards, I do not recollect seeing any living creature in that garden during our stay, except a little frowsy wad of a dog, which dashed into our premises one morning, and seizing on a large piece of sponge made off with it up the Pincian Hill. If that sponge fell to the lot of some time-encrusted Romanese, and Providence was merciful enough to inspire him with a conception of its proper use, it cannot be said of the little Skye terrier that he lived in vain.

If no other feet than ours invaded those neatly-gravelled walks, causing the shy, silvery lizards to retreat swiftly to the borders of the flower-beds or behind the corpulent green tubs holding the fan-palms, we were keenly conscious now and then of being overlooked. On pleasant afternoons lines of carriages and groups of gayly-dressed people went winding up the steep road which, skirted with ilexes and pines and mimosa bushes, leads to the popular promenade of the Pincio. There, if anywhere, you get a breath of fresh air in the heated term, and always the most magnificent view of the city and its environs. There, of old, were the gardens of Lucullus ; there Messalina, with sinful good taste, had her pleasure-house, and held her Satur-

nalia; and there, to-day, the band of Victor Emmanuel plays twice a week in the
sunset, luring thither all the sunny belles
and beaux of Rome. Monte Pincio, as I
have said, sloped down on one side to our
garden. On the crest of the hill command-
ing our demesne was a low wall of masonry.
From time to time a killing Roman fop
would come and lean in an elegant attitude
against this wall, nursing himself on the
ivory ball of his cane, and staring unblush-
ingly at the blonde-haired lady sitting under her own hired fig-tree in the hotel garden. What a fascinating creature he was,
with his little black mustache, almost as
heavy as a pencil mark, his olive skin, his
wide, effeminate eyes, his slender rattan
figure, and his cameo sleeve-studs! What
a sad dog he was, to melt into those lan-
guishing postures up there, and let loose
all those facile blandishments, careless of
the heart-break he must inevitably cause
the simple American *signora* in the gar-

den below! We used to glance up at this gilded youth from time to time, and it was a satisfaction to reflect what an ineffable idiot he was, like all his kind in every land under the sun.

This was our second sojourn in Rome, and we had spent two industrious weeks, picking up the threads of the Past, dropped temporarily in April in order to run down and explore Naples before Southern Italy became too hot to hold us: two busy weeks, into which were crowded visits to the catacombs and the Baths of Caracalla, and excursions on the Campagna — at this time of year a vast red sea of poppies strewn with the wrecks of ancient tombs; we had humiliated our nostrils in strolling through the Ghetto, and gladdened our eyes daily with the bronze equestrian statue of Marcus Aurelius in the Piazza del Campidoglio; we had made a pilgrimage to the Abbey alle Tre Fontane, and regarded with a proper sense of awe the three fountains

which had gushed forth at the points where
the head of the Apostle Paul landed, in
those three eccentric leaps it accomplished
after his execution; we had breathed the
musky air of Santa Maria Maggiore and the
Basilica San Paolo, and once, by chance,
on a minor *fête* day, lighted on a pretty
pageant in St. John Lateran; we had
looked our fill of statuary and painting,
and jasper and lapis-lazuli; we had bur-
rowed under the Eternal City in crypt and
dungeon, and gazed down upon it from the
dizzy Lantern of St. Peter's. The blight-
ing summer was at hand; the phantasmal
malaria was stalking the Campagna at
night: it was time to go. There was nothing more to be done in Rome unless we did
the Roman fever — nothing but that, indeed, if we were not inclined to pay a visit
to a Certain Old Gentleman. This alternative appeared to have so many advantages over the Roman fever that it at once
took the shape of an irresistible temptation.

At least it did to Madama and me, but the other pilgrim of the party was of a more reflective mind, and was disposed to look at the question judicially. He was not going to call on a Certain Old Gentleman as if he were a frescoed panel in the Sistine Chapel; it was not fair to put a human being on the same footing as a nameless heathen statue dug out of the cinders of Pompeii; the statue could not complain, and would be quite in the wrong if it did complain, at being treated as a curiosity; but the human being might, and had a perfect right to protest. H——'s objections to the visit were so numerous and so warmly put, that Madama and I were satisfied that he had made up his mind to go.

"However, the gentleman is not adverse to receiving strangers, as I understand it," said H——, imperceptibly weakening.

"On the contrary," I said, "it is one of the relaxations of his old age, and he is especially hospitable to our countrymen. A great many Americans" —

"Then let us go, by all means," inter-
rupted Madama. "Among the Romans
one should do — as Americans do."

"Only much better," I suggested. "I
have sometimes been not proud of my countrymen on this side of the water. The De-
laneys in the Borghese Gallery, the other
day! I almost longed for the intervention
of the Inquisition. If it had been in Venice and in the fifteenth century, I'd have
dropped an anonymous communication into
the letter-box of the Palace of the Doges,
and had the Council of Ten down on Miss
Fanny Delaney in no time."

"The chances are he is out of town,"
said Madama, ignoring my vindictiveness.

"He has a summer residence near Al-
bano," said H——, "but he never goes
there now; at least he has not occupied the
villa for the last few years, in fact, not
since 1870."

"Where does he pass his summers,
then?" asked Madama.

6

" In Rome."

" How eccentric ! "

" I suppose he has his weak points, like the rest of us," said H——, charitably.

" He ought to have his strong points, to endure the summer in Rome, with the malaria, and the sirocco, and the typhoon, and all the dreadful things that befall."

" The typhoon, my dear " —

Though the discussion did not end here that May evening on the steps of the hotel-garden, it ends here in my record ; it being sufficient for the reader to know that we then and there resolved to undertake the visit in question.   The scribe of the party dispatched a note to Signor V—— expressing a desire to pay our respects to his venerable friend before we left town, and begging that an early day, if any, be appointed for the interview.   Signor V—— was an Italian acquaintance of ours who carried a diplomatic key that fitted almost any lock.

We breakfasted betimes, the next morn-

ing, and sat lingering over our coffee, awaiting Signor V——'s reply to our note. The
reply had so impressive an air of not coming, that we fell to planning an excursion
to Tivoli, and had ordered a carriage to
that end, when Stefano appeared, bearing
an envelope on his silver-plated waiter. (I
think Stefano was born with that waiter in
his hand ; he never laid it down for a moment ; if any duty obliged him to use both
hands, he clapped the waiter under his arm
or between his knees ; I used to fancy that
it was attached to his body by some mysterious, invisible ligament, the severing of
which would have caused his instant disso-
lution.) Signor V—— advised us that his
venerable friend would be gracious enough
to receive us that very day at one half-hour
after noon. In a postscript the signor in-
timated that the gentlemen would be expected to wear evening dress, *minus* gloves,
and that it was imperative on the part of
Madama to be costumed completely in

black and to wear only a black veil on her hair. Such was one of the whims of a Certain Old Gentleman.

Here a dilemma arose. Among Madama's wardrobe there was no costume of this lugubrious description. The nearest approach to it was a statuesque black robe, elaborately looped and covered with agreeable arabesques of turquoise-blue silk. There was nothing to do but to rip off these celestial trimmings, and they were ripped off, though it went against the woman-heart. Poor, vain little silk dress, that had never been worn, what swift retribution overtook you for being nothing but artistic, and graceful, and lovely, and — Parisian, which includes all blessed adjectives!

From the bottom of a trunk in which they had lain since we left London, H—— and I exhumed our dress-coats. Though perfectly new (like their amiable sister, the black silk gown), they came out looking remarkably aged. They had inexplicable bulges in the back, as if they had been worn by somebody with six or eight shoulder-blades, and were covered all over in front with minute wrinkles, recalling the famous portrait of the late Mr. Parr in his hundred and fiftieth year. H—— and I got into our creased elegance with not more intemperate comment than might be pardoned, and repaired to the parlor, where we found Madama arranging a voluminous veil of inky crape over her hair, and regarding herself in a full-length mirror with gloomy satisfaction. The carriage was at the *porte cochère*, and we departed, stealing silently through the deserted hotel corridor, and looking for all the world, I imagine, like a couple of rascally undertakers making off with a nun.

II.

We had been so expeditious in our preparations that on seating ourselves in the
carriage we found much superfluous time
on our hands; so we went around Robin
Hood's barn to our destination — a delightful method in Rome — taking the Cenci
Palace and the Hilda's Tower of Hawthorne's romance in our impartial sweep,
and stopping at a shop in the Piazza di
Spagna, where Madama purchased an amber rosary for only about three times as
many *lire* as she need have paid for it anywhere else on the globe. If an Italian shop-
keeper should be submitted to a chemical
analysis, and his rascality carefully sepa-
rated from the other ingredients and thrown
away, there would be nothing left of him.
I think it is Dumas *fils* who remarks that

the ancients had but one god for shop-
keepers and thieves.

There were not many persons to be seen
in the streets. It was nearing the hour
when Rome keeps in-doors and takes its
ease ; besides, it was out of season, as I
have stated, and the Gaul and the Briton,
and the American savage with his bowie-
knife and revolver, had struck a trail north-
ward. At the church portals, to be sure,
was the usual percentage of distressing beggars — the old hag out of Macbeth, who
insists on lifting the padded leather door-
screen for you, the one-eyed man, the one-
armed man, the one-legged man, and other
fragments. The poor you have always with
you, in Italy. They lash themselves, metaphorically, to the spokes of your carriage-
wheel, and go round with you.

Ever since our second arrival in Rome
the population seemed to have been undergoing a process of evaporation. From the
carriage-window we now and then caught

sight of a sandalled monk flitting by in the shadow of a tall building — the sole human thing that appears to be in a hurry in this stagnant city. His furtive air betrays his consciousness that he is only tolerated where he once ruled nearly supreme. It is an evil time for him; his tenure is brief. Now that the government has unearthed him, he is fading out like a Pompeian fresco. As he glides by, there in the shade, with the aspect of a man belated on some errand of vital import, I have an idea he is not going anywhere in particular. Before these doleful days had befallen the Church of Rome, every third figure you met was a gray-cowled friar, or a white-robed Dominican, or a shovel-hatted reverend father looking like a sharp raven; but they all are rare birds now, and, for the most part, the few that are left stick to their perches in the stricken, mouldy old monasteries and convents, shedding their feathers and wasting away hour by hour, the last of the brood!

In the vicinity of Trajan's Column we encountered a bewildered-looking goat-herd, who had strayed in from the Campagna, perhaps with some misty anticipation that the Emperor Nero had a fresh lot of choice Christians to be served up that day in the arena of the Coliseum. I wondered if this rustic wore those pieces of hairy goatskin laced to his calves in July and August. It threw one into a perspiration to look at him. But I forgave him on inspection, for with his pointed hat, through an aperture of which his hair had run to seed, and his scarlet sash, and his many-colored tattered habiliments, he was the only bit of picturesque costume we saw in Rome. Picturesque costume is a thing of the past there, except those fraudulent remains of it that hang about the studios in the Via Margutta, or at the steps of the Trinita de' Monti, on the shoulders of professional models.

Even the Corso was nearly deserted and

quite dull this day, and it is scarcely gay when it is thronged, as we saw it early in the spring. Possibly it is lively during the Carnival. It would need masking and music and illumination to lift its gloom, in spite of its thousand balconies. The sense of antiquity and the heavy, uncompromising architecture of Rome oppress one painfully until one comes to love her. My impression of Rome is something so solid and tangible that I have felt at times as if I could pack it in a box, like a bas-relief, or a statue, or a segment of a column, and send it home by the Cunard line. Compared with the airiness and grace and color of other Continental cities, Rome is dull. The arcades of Bologna and the dingy streets of Verona and Padua are not duller.

If I linger by the way, and seem in no haste to get to a Certain Old Gentleman, it is because the Roman atmosphere has in it some medicinal property that induces reverie and procrastination, and relaxes the

sinews of effort. I wonder where Caligula
found the enterprise to torture his victims,
and Brutus the vivacity to stab Cæsar.

Our zigzag route brought us back to the
Piazza del Popolo, from which we turned
into the Via Ripetta on the left, and rat-
tled over the stone pavement past the Castle of St. Angelo, towards St. Peter's. It
was not until the horses slackened their
speed, and finally stood still in a spacious
cortile at the foot of a wide flight of stone
steps, that our purpose dropped a certain
fantastic aspect it had worn, and became a
serious if not a solemn business. Notwith-
standing our deliberations over the matter
at the hotel, I think I had not fully real-
ized that in proposing to visit a Certain
Old Gentleman we were proposing to visit
the Pope of Rome.[1] The proposition had
seemed all along like a piece of mild pleas-

[1] Since this paper was written, Pius IX., Cardinal Antonelli, and King Victor Emmanuel have laid down the burden
of life. These distinguished personages seem to have con-
spired to render my note-book obsolete.

antry, as if one should say, "I think I'll
drop round on Titus Flavius in the course
of the forenoon," or "I've half a mind to
look in on Cicero and Pompey, and see
how they feel this morning after their little
dissipation last night at the villa of Lucullus." The Pope of Rome — not the Pope
regnant, but the Pope of Rome in the abstract — had up to that hour presented
himself to my mental eye as an august
spectacular figure - head, belonging to no
particular period, who might turn out after
all to be an ingenious historical fiction per-
petrated by the same humorist that invented Pocahontas. The Pope of Rome!
— he had been as vague to me as Adam
and as improbable as Noah.

But there stood Signor V—— at the car-
riage-step, waiting to conduct us into the
Vatican, and there, on either side of the
portals at the head of the massive staircase, lounged two of the papal guard in that
jack - of - diamonds costume which Michael

Angelo designed for them — in the way of
a practical joke, I fancy. They held hal-
berds in their hands, these mediæval gentlemen, and it was a mercy they did n't chop
us to pieces as we passed between them.
What an absurd uniform for a man-at-arms
of the nineteenth century ! These fellows,
clad in rainbow, suggested a pair of harle-
quins out of a Christmas pantomime. Farther on we came to more stone staircase,
and more stupid papal guard with melodra-
matic battle-axes, and were finally ushered
into a vast, high - studded chamber at the
end of a much-stuccoed corridor.

Coming as we did out of the blinding
sunshine, this chamber seemed to us at first
but a gloomy cavern. It was so poorly
lighted by numerous large windows on the
western side that several seconds elapsed
before we could see anything distinctly.
One or two additional windows would have
made it quite dark. At the end of the
apartment, near the door at which we had

entered, was a dais with three tawdry rococo gilt arm-chairs, having for background an enormous painting of the Virgin, but by what master I was unable to make out. The draperies of the room were of some heavy dark stuff, a green rep, if I remember, and the floor was covered with a thick carpet through which the solid stone flagging beneath repelled the pressure of your foot. There was a singular absence of color everywhere, of that mosaic work and Renaissance gilding with which the eyes soon become good friends in Italy. The frescoes of the ceiling, if there were any frescoes, were in some shy neutral tint, and did not introduce themselves to us. On the right, at the other extremity of the room, was a double door, which led, as we were correct in supposing, to the private apartments of the Pope.

Presently our eyes grew reconciled to the semi-twilight, which seemed to have been transported hither with a faint spicy odor of incense from some ancient basilica — a proper enough light for an audience-chamber in the Vatican. Fixed against the wall on either side, and extending nearly the entire length of the room, was a broad settee, the greater part of which was already occupied when we entered. Formerly women were not allowed a public audience with the Pope. Madame Junot, in giving in her Mémoires an account of her interview with Pius VII., says: "Whenever a woman is presented to the Pope, it must be so managed as to have the appearance of accident. Women are not admitted into the Vatican, but his Holiness permits them to be presented to him in the Sistine Chapel, or in his promenades. But the meeting must always appear to be the effect of chance." I do not know when this custom fell into desuetude; possibly long before the reign of Pius IX. The majority of the persons now present were women.

Signor V—— stationed himself at our side, and began a conversation with H—— on the troubles that had overtaken and the perils that still menaced the True Church. The disintegration of nunneries and monasteries and the closing up of religious houses had been fraught with much individual suffering. Hundreds of simple, learned men had been suddenly thrust out into a world of which they had no knowledge and where they were as helpless as so many infants. In some instances the government had laid hands on strictly private properties, on funds contributed by private persons to establish asylums for women of noble birth in reduced circumstances — portionless daughters and cousins desirous of leading a life of pious meditation and seclusion. Many of these institutions possessed enormous revenues, and were strong temptations to the Italian government, whose money-chest gave out a pathetically hollow sound when tapped against in 1870.

One does not need to be a Catholic to perceive the injustice of this kind of seizure; one's sympathy may go forth with the unhoused nuns: as to the monks — it does not hurt any man to earn his own living. The right and the necessity to work ought to be regarded as a direct blessing from God by men who, for these many centuries, have had their stomachs "with good capon lined," chiefly at the expense of the poor.

Conversation had become general; every one spoke in a subdued tone, and a bee-like hum rose and fell on the air. With the exception of a neat little body, with her husband, at our right, the thirty or forty persons present were either French, German, English, Russian, or Italian.

I remarked to Signor V—— on the absence of the American element, and attributed it to the lateness of the season.

"That does not wholly explain it," said Signor V——. "There were numberless applications from Americans to attend this

7

reception, but his Holiness just at present is not inclined to receive many Americans."

" Why not? "

" A few weeks ago, his Holiness was treated with great disrespect by an American, a lawyer from one of your Western States, I believe, who did not rise from his seat or kneel when the Pope entered the room."

" He ought to have risen, certainly; but is it imperative that one should kneel? "

" It is; but then, it is not imperative on any one to be presented to his Holiness. If the gentleman did not wish to conform to the custom, he ought to have stayed away."

" He might have been ignorant of that phase of the ceremony," said I, with a sudden poignant sense of sympathy with my unhappy countryman. "What befell him? "

" He was courteously escorted from the chamber by the gentleman in waiting,"

said Signor V——, glancing at an official
near the door, who looked as if he were a
cross between a divinity student and a policeman.

It occurred to me that few things would
be less entertaining than to be led out of
this audience-chamber in the face and eyes
of France, Germany, Russia, and Italy —
in the face and eyes of the civilized world,
in fact; for would not the next number of
Galignani's Messenger have a paragraph
about it? I had supposed that Catholics
knelt to the Pope, as a matter of course,
but that Protestants were exempt from pay-
ing this homage, on the same ground that
Quakers are not expected to remove their
hats like other folk. I wondered what
Friend Eli would do, if destiny dropped
him into the midst of one of the receptions
of Pius IX. However, it was somewhat
late to go to the bottom of the matter, so I
dismissed it from my mind, and began an
examination of my neighbors.

A cynic has observed that all cats are gray in the twilight. He said cats, but meant women. I am convinced that all women are not alike in a black silk dress, very simply trimmed and with no color about it except a white rose at the corsage. There are women — perhaps not too many — whose beauty is heightened by an austere toilette. Such a one was the lady opposite me, with her veil twisted under her chin and falling negligently over the left shoulder. The beauty of her face flashed out like a diamond from its sombre setting. She had the brightest of dark eyes, with such a thick, long fringe of dark eyelashes that her whole countenance turned into night when she drooped her eyelids; when she lifted them, it was morning again. As if to show us what might be done in the manner of contrasts, nature had given this lady some newly coined Roman gold for hair. I think Eve was that way — both blonde and brunette. My *vis-à-vis* would have been gracious in any costume, but I am positive that nothing would have gone so well with her as the black silk dress, fitting closely to the pliant bust and not losing a single line or curve. As she sat, turned three quarters face, the window behind her threw the outlines of her slender figure into sharp relief. The lady herself was perfectly well aware of it.

Next to this charming person was a substantial English matron, who wore her hair done up in a kind of turret, and looked like a lithograph of a distant view of Windsor Castle. She sat bolt upright, and formed, if I may say so, the initial letter of a long line of fascinatingly ugly women. Imagine a row of Sphinxes in deep mourning. It would have been an unbroken line of feminine severity, but for a handsome young priest with a strikingly spiritual face, who came in, like a happy word in parenthesis, half-way down the row. I soon exhausted the resources of this part of the room; my

eyes went back to the Italian lady so prettily framed in the embrasure of the window,
and would have lingered there had I not
got interested in an old gentleman seated
on my left.   When he came into the room,
blinking his kindly blue eyes and rubbing
his hands noiselessly together and beaming
benevolently on everybody, just as if he
were expected, I fell in love with him.
His fragile, aristocratic hands appeared to
have been done up by the same *blanchis-
seuse* who did his linen, which was as white
and crisp as an Alpine snow-drift, as were
also two wintry strands of hair artfully
trained over either ear.   Otherwise he was
as bald and shiny as a glacier.   He seated
himself with an old-fashioned, courteous
bow to the company assembled, and a pro-
testing wave of the hand, as if to say,
" Good people, I pray you, do not disturb
yourselves," and made all that side of the
room bright with his smiling.   He looked
so clean and sweet, just such a wholesome

figure as one would like to have at one's
fireside as grandfather, that I began formu-
lating the wish that I might, thirty or forty
years hence, be taken for his twin brother;
when a neighbor of his created a distur-
bance.

This neighbor was a young Italian lady
or gentleman — I cannot affirm which — of
perhaps ten months' existence, who up to
the present time had been asleep in the
arms of its *bonne*. Awaking suddenly, the
bambino had given vent to the shrillest
shrieks, impelled thereto by the strange-
ness of the surrounding features, or perhaps
by some conscientious scruples about being
in the Vatican. I picked out the mother
at once by the worried expression that flew
to the countenance of a lady near me, and
in a gentleman who instantly assumed an
air of having no connection whatever with
the baleful infant, I detected the father. I
do not remember to have seen a stronger
instance of youthful depravity and dupli-

city than that lemon-colored child afforded.
The moment the nurse walked with it, it
sunk into the sweetest of slumber, and
peace settled upon its little nose like a
drowsy bee upon the petal of a flower; but
the instant the *bonne* made a motion to sit
down, it broke forth again. I do not know
what ultimately befell the vocal goblin;
possibly it was collared by the lieutenant
of the guard outside, and thrown into the
deepest dungeon of the palace; at all events
it disappeared after the announcement that
his Holiness would be with us shortly.
Whatever virtues Pius IX. possessed, punc-
tuality was not one of them, for he had
kept us waiting three quarters of an hour,
and we had still another fifteen minutes to
wait.

The monotonous hum of conversation
hushed itself abruptly, the two sections of
the wide door I have mentioned were
thrown open, and the Pope, surrounded by
his cardinals and a number of foreign

princes, entered. The occupants of the
two long settees rose, and then, as if they
were automata worked by the same tyran-
nical wire, sunk simultaneously into an attitude of devotion. For an instant I was
seized with a desperate desire not to kneel.
There is something in an American knee,
when it is rightly constructed, that makes
it an awkward thing to kneel with before
any man born of woman. Perhaps, if the
choice were left one, either to prostrate
one's self before a certain person or be shot,
one might make a point of it — and be shot.
But that was not the alternative in the
present case. If I had failed to follow the
immemorial custom I should not have had
the honor of a fusilade, but would have
been ignominiously led away by one of
those highly-colored Swiss guards, and, in
my dress suit, would have presented to the
general stare the appearance of a preten-
tious ace of spades being wiped out by a gay
right-bower. Such humiliation was not to

be thought of! So, wishing myself safely back amid the cruder civilization of the New World, and with a mental protest accompanied by a lofty compassion for the weakness and cowardice of human-kind, I slid softly down with the rest of the miserable sinners. I was in the very act, when I was chilled to the marrow by catching a sidelong glimpse of my benign old gentleman placidly leaning back in his seat, with his hands folded over his well-filled waistcoat and that same benevolent smile petrified on his countenance. He was fast asleep.

Immediately a tall, cadaverous person in a scant, funereal garment emerged from somewhere, and touched the sleeper on the shoulder. The old gentleman unclosed his eyes slowly and with difficulty, and was so far from taking in the situation that he made a gesture as if to shake hands with the tall, cadaverous person. Then it all flashed upon the dear old boy, and he dropped to his knees with so comical and despairing an air of contrition that the presence of forty thousand popes would not have prevented me from laughing.

Another discomposing incident occurred at this juncture. Two removes below me was a smooth-faced German of gigantic stature; he must have been six or seven inches over six feet in height, but so absurdly short between the knee-cap and ankle that as he knelt he towered head and shoulders above us all, resembling a great, overgrown school-boy, standing up as straight as he could. It was so he impressed one of the ghostly attendants, who advanced quickly towards him with the evident purpose of requesting him to kneel. Discovering his error just in time, the reverend father retreated, much abashed.

All eyes were now turned toward the Pope and his suite, and this trifling episode passed unnoticed save by two or three individuals in the immediate neighborhood,

who succeeded in swallowing their smiles,
but did not dare glance at each other afterwards.   The Pope advanced to the centre
of the upper end of the room, leaning heavily on his ivory-handled cane, the princes
in black and the cardinals in scarlet standing behind him in picturesque groups, like
the chorus in an opera.   Indeed, it was all
like a scene on the stage.   There was
something premeditated and spectacular
about it, as if these persons had been engaged for the occasion.   Several of the
princes were Russian, with names quite
well adapted to not being remembered.
Among the Italian gentlemen was Cardinal Nobli Vatteleschi — he was not a cardinal then, by the way — who died not
long ago.

Within whispering distance of the Pope
stood Cardinal Antonelli — a man who
would not escape observation in any assem-
bly of notable personages.   If the Inquisition should be revived in its early genial

form, and the reader should fall into its
hands — as would very likely be the case,
if a branch office were established in this
country — he would feel scarcely comfortable if his chief inquisitor had so cold and
subtle a countenance as Giacome Antonelli's.

We occasionally meet in political or in
social life a man whose presence seems to
be an anachronism — a man belonging to a
type we fancied extinct ; he affects us as a
living dodo would the naturalist, though
perhaps not with so great an enthusiasm.
Cardinal Antonelli, in his bearing and the
cast of his countenance, had that air of re-
moteness which impresses us in the works
of the old masters. I had seen somewhere
a head of Velasquez for which the cardinal
might have posed. With the subdued afternoon light falling upon him through the
deep-set lunette, he seemed like some cruel
prelate escaped from one of the earlier volumes of Froude's History of England —

subtle, haughty, intolerant. I did not mean to allow so sinister an impression to remain on my mind; but all I have since read and heard of Cardinal Antonelli has not obliterated it.

It was a pleasure to turn from the impassible prime minister to the gentle and altogether interesting figure of his august master, with his small, sparkling eyes, remarkably piercing when he looked at you point-blank, and a smile none the less winsome that it lighted up a mouth denoting unusual force of will. His face was not at all the face of a man who had passed nearly half a century in arduous diplomatic and ecclesiastical labors; it was certainly the face of a man who had led a temperate, blameless private life, in noble contrast to many of his profligate predecessors, whom the world was only too glad to have snugly stowed away in their gorgeous porphyry coffins with a marble mistress carved atop.

Giovanni Maria Mastai Ferretti was born

in Sinigaglia on the 13th of May, 1792; the week previous to this reception he had celebrated his eighty-third birthday; but he did not look over sixty-five or seventy, as he stood there in his skull-cap of cream-white broadcloth and his long pontifical robes of the same material — a costume that lent an appearance of height to an undersized, stoutly built figure. With his silvery hair straggling from beneath the skull-cap, and his smoothly-shaven pale face, a trifle heavy, perhaps because of the double chin, he was a very beautiful old man. After pausing a moment or two in the middle of the chamber, and taking a bird's-eye glance at his guests, the Pope began his rounds. Assigned to each group of five or ten persons was an official who presented the visitors by name, indicating their nationality, station, etc. So far as the nationality was involved, that portion of the introduction was obviously superfluous, for the Pope singled out his countrymen at a glance, and at once addressed them in Italian, scarcely waiting for the master of ceremonies to perform his duties. To foreigners his Holiness spoke in French. After a few words of salutation he gave his hand to each person, who touched it with his lips or his forehead, or simply retained it an instant. It was a deathly cold hand, on the forefinger of which was a great seal ring bearing a mottled gray stone that seemed frozen. As the Pope moved slowly along, devotees caught at the hem of his robe and pressed it to their lips, and in most instances bowed down and kissed his feet. I suppose it was only by years of practice that his Holiness was able to avoid stepping on a nose here and there.

It came our turn at last. As he approached us he said, with a smile, " Ah, I see you are Americans." Signor V—— then presented us formally, and the Pope was kind enough to say to us what he had probably said to twenty thousand other

Americans in the course of several hundred similar occasions. After he had passed on, the party that had paid their respects to him resumed their normal position — I am not sure this was not the most enjoyable feature of the affair — and gave themselves up to watching the other presentations. When these were concluded, the Pope returned to the point of his departure, and proceeded to bless the rosaries and crosses and souvenirs that had been brought, in greater or lesser numbers, by every one. There were salvers piled with rosaries, arms strung from wrist to shoulder with rosaries — so many carven amulets, and circlets of beads and crucifixes, indeed, that it would have been the labor of weeks to bless them separately; so his Holiness blessed them in bulk.

It was then that the neat little American lady who sat next us confirmed my suspicions as to her brideship by slyly slipping from her wedding finger a plain gold

8

ring, which she attached to her rosary with
a thread from her veil. Seeing herself detected in the act, she turned to Madama,
and, making up the most piquant little
face in the world, whispered confidentially,
" Of course I 'm not a Roman Catholic, you
know; but if there 's anything efficacious
in the blessing, I don't want to lose it. I
want to take *all* the chances." For my
part, I hope and believe the Pope's blessing will cling to that diminutive wedding
ring for many and many a year.

This ceremony finished, his Holiness addressed to his guests the neatest of fare-
wells, delivered in enviable French, in
which he wished a prosperous voyage to
those pilgrims whose homes lay beyond the
sea, and a happy return to all. When he
touched, as he did briefly, on the misfor-
tunes of the church, an adorable fire came
into his eyes; fifty of his eighty-three win-
ters slipped from him as if by enchantment,
and for a few seconds he stood forth in the

prime of life. He spoke some five or seven
minutes, and nothing could have been more
dignified and graceful than the matter and
the manner of his words. The benediction
was followed by a general rustle and movement among the princes and *eminenze* at the
farther end of the room ; the double door
opened softly, and closed — and that was
the last the Pope saw of us.

VI.

ON A BALCONY.

VI.

ON A BALCONY.

I.

A BALCONY, as we northerns know it, is a humiliating architectural link between in-doors and out-of-doors. To be on a balcony is to be nowhere in particular: you are not exactly at home, and yet cannot be described as out; your privacy and your freedom are alike sacrificed. The approaching bore has you at his mercy; he can draw a bead on you with his rifled eye at a hundred paces. You may gaze abstractedly at a cloud, or turn your back, but you cannot escape him, though the chance is always open to you to drop a bureau on him as he lifts his hand to the bell-knob. One could fill a volume with a condensed catalogue of

the inconveniences of an average balcony.
But when the balcony hangs from the
third-story window of an Old World palace,
and when the façade of that Old World
palace looks upon the Bay of Naples, you
had better think twice before you speak
depreciatingly of balconies. With that
sheet of mysteriously blue water in front
of you; with Mount Vesuvius moodily
smoking his perpetual calumet on your
left; with the indented shore sweeping towards Pozzuoli and Baiæ on your right;
with Capri and Ischia notching the ashen
gray line of the horizon; with the tender
heaven of May bending over all — with
these accessories, I say, it must be con-
ceded that one might be very much worse
off in this world than on a balcony.

I know that I came to esteem the narrow
iron-grilled shelf suspended from my bedroom window in the hotel on the Strada
Chiatamone as the choicest spot in all Naples. After a ramble through the unsavory

streets it was always a pleasure to get back
to it, and I think I never in my life did a
more sensible thing in the department of
pure idleness than when I resolved to spend
an entire day on that balcony. One morning, after an early breakfast, I established
myself there in an arm-chair placed beside
a small table holding a couple of books, a
paper of cigarettes, and a field-glass. My
companions had gone to explore the pic-
ture-galleries; but I had my picture-gallery
chez moi — in the busy *strada* below, in the
villa-fringed bay, in the cluster of yellow-
roofed little towns clinging to the purple
slopes of Mount Vesuvius and patiently
awaiting annihilation. The beauty of Naples lies along its water-front, and from my
coigne of vantage I had nothing to desire.

If the Bay of Naples had not been described a million times during the present
century, I should still not attempt to describe it: I have made a discovery which
no other traveller seems to have made —

that its loveliness is untranslatable. More-
over, enthusiasm is not permitted to the
modern tourist. He may be æsthetic, or
historic, or scientific, or analytic, or didac-
tic, or any kind of ic, except enthusiastic.
He may be Meissonier-like in his detail;
he may give you the very tint and texture
of a honeycombed frieze over a Byzantine
gateway, or lay bare the yet faintly palpi-
tating heart of some old-time tragedy, but
he must do it in a nonchalant, pulseless
manner, with a semi-supercilious elevation
of nostril. He would lose his self-respect
if he were to be deeply moved by anything,
or really interested in anything.

> " All that he sees in Bagdad
> Is the Tigris to float him away."

He is the very antipode of his elder brother
of fifty years syne, who used to go about
filling his note-book with Thoughts on
Standing at the Tomb of Marcus Antoni-
nus, Emotions on Finding a Flea on my
Shirt Collar in the Val d'Arno, and the

like. The latter-day tourist is a great deal
less innocent, but is he more amusing than
those old-fashioned sentimental travellers
who had at least freshness of sympathies
and never dreamed of trying to pass themselves off as cynics? Dear, ingenuous, im-
pressible souls — peace to your books of
travel! May they line none but trunks
destined to prolonged foreign tours, or those
thrice happy trunks which go on bridal
journeys!

At the risk of being relegated to the
footing of those emotional ancients, I am
going to confess to an unrequited passion
for Mount Vesuvius. Never was passion
less regarded by its object. I did not aspire to be received with the warmth of
manner that characterized its reception of
the elder Pliny in the year 79, but I did
want Mount Vesuvius to pay me a little attention, which it might easily have done —
without putting itself out. On arriving
in town I had called on Mount Vesuvius.

The acquaintance rested there. Every night, after my candle was extinguished, I stood a while at the open window and glanced half-expectantly across the bay; but the sullen monster made no sign. That slender spiral column of smoke, spreading out like a toad-stool on attaining a certain height, but neither increasing nor diminishing in volume, lifted itself into the starlight. Sometimes I fancied that the smoke had taken a deeper lurid tinge; but it was only fancy. How I longed for a sudden burst of flame and scoriæ from those yawning jaws!— for one awful instant's illumination of the bay and the shipping and the picturesque villages asleep at the foot of the mountain! I did not care to have the spectacle last more than four or five heartbeats at the longest; but it was a thing worth wishing for.

I do not believe that even the most hardened traveller is able wholly to throw off the grim fascination of Mount Vesuvius so long as he is near it; and I quite understand the potency of the spell which has led the poor people of Resina to set up their Lares and Penates on cinder-buried Herculaneum. Bide your time, O Resina, and Portici, and Torre del Greco! The doom of Pompeii and Herculaneum shall yet be yours. "If it be now, 't is not to come; if it be not to come, it will be now; if it be not now, yet it *will* come."

Indeed, these villages have suffered repeatedly in ancient and modern times. In the eruption of 1631 seven torrents of lava swept down the mountain, taking in their course Bosco, Torre dell' Annunziata, Torre del Greco, Resina, and Portici, and destroying three thousand lives. That calamity and later though not so terrible catastrophes have not prevented the people from rebuilding on the old sites. The singular fertility of the soil around the base of the volcanic pile lures them back — or is it that they are under the influence of that nameless glamour I have hinted at? Perhaps those half-indistinguishable shapes of petrified gnome and satyr and glyptodon which lie tumbled in heaps all about this region have something to do with it. It would be easy to believe that some of the nightmare figures and landscapes in Doré's illustrations of The Wandering Jew were suggested to the artist by the fantastic forms in which the lava streams have cooled along the flanks of Vesuvius.

A man might spend a busy life in studying the phenomena of this terrible mountain. It is undergoing constant changes. The paths to the crater have to be varied from month to month, so it is never safe to make the ascent without a guide. There is a notable sympathy existing between the volcanoes of Vesuvius and Ætna, although seventy miles apart; when one is in a period of unusual activity, the other, as a rule, remains quiescent. May be the imprisoned giant Enceladus works both forges.

I never think of either mountain without
recalling Longfellow's poem : —

"Under Mount Ætna he lies,
    It is slumber, it is not death;
For he struggles at times to arise,
And above him the lurid skies
    Are hot with his fiery breath.

"The crags are piled on his breast,
    The earth is heaped on his head;
But the groans of his wild unrest,
Though smothered and half suppressed,
    Are heard, and he is not dead.

"And the nations far away
    Are watching with eager eyes;
They talk together and say,
'To-morrow, perhaps to-day,
    Enceladus will arise!'

"And the old gods, the austere
    Oppressors in their strength,
Stand aghast and white with fear
At the ominous sounds they hear,
    And tremble, and mutter, 'At length!'

"Ah me! for the land that is sown
    With the harvest of despair!
Where the burning cinders, blown

From the lips of the overthrown
   Enceladus, fill the air.

" Where ashes are heaped in drifts
   Over vineyard and field and town,
Whenever he starts and lifts
His head through the blackened rifts
   Of the crags that keep him down.

" See, see ! the red light shines !
   'T is the glare of his awful eyes !
And the storm-wind shouts through the pines,
Of Alps and of Apennines,
   ' Enceladus, arise ! ' "

For the first half hour after I had stationed myself on the balcony, that morning, I kept my glass turned pretty constantly in the direction of Mount Vesuvius, trying to make out the *osteria* at the Hermitage, where we had halted one noon to drink some doubtful Lachryma Christi and eat a mysterious sort of ragout, composed — as one of our party suggested — of missing-link. Whether or not the small inn had shifted its position over night, I was unable to get a focus upon it. In the mean while

I myself, in my oriole nest overhanging the strada, had become an object of burning interest to sundry persons congregated below. I was suddenly aware that three human beings were standing in the middle of the carriage-way with their faces turned up to the balcony. The first was a slender, hideous girl, with large eyes and little clothing, who held out a tambourine, the rattle-snake-like clatter of which had attracted my attention; next to her stood a fellow with canes and palm-leaf fans; then came a youth loaded down with diminutive osier baskets of Naples strawberries, which look, and as for that matter taste, like tufts of red worsted. This select trio was speedily turned into a quartette by the arrival of a sea-faring gentleman, who bore on his head a tray of boiled crabs, sea-urchins, and small fried fish — *frutti di mare*. As a fifth personage approached, with possibly the arithmetical intention of adding himself to the line, I sent the whole party off with a wave of the hand; that is to say, I waved to them to go, but they merely retired to the curb-stone opposite the hotel, and sat down.

The last comer, perhaps disdaining to associate himself too closely with vulgar persons engaged in trade, leaned indolently against the sea-wall behind them, and stared at me in a vacant, dreamy fashion. He was a handsome wretch, physically. Praxiteles might have carved him. I have no doubt that his red Phrygian cap concealed a pair of pointed furry ears; but his tattered habiliments and the strips of gay cloth wound, brigand-like, about his calves were not able to hide the ungyved grace of his limbs. The upturned face was for the moment as empty of expression as a cipher, but I felt that it was capable, on occasion, of expressing almost any depth of cunning and dare-devil ferocity. I dismissed the idea of the Dancing Faun. It was Masaniello — Masaniello ruined by good government and the dearth of despots.

The girl with the tambourine was not in business by herself; she was the familiar of a dark-browed organ-man, who now made his appearance, holding in one hand a long fishing-line baited with monkey. On observing that this line was too short to reach me, the glance of despair and reproach which the pirate cast up at the balcony was comical. Nevertheless he proceeded to turn the crank of his music-mill, while the girl — whose age I estimated at anywhere between sixteen and sixty — executed the tarantella in a disinterested manner on the sidewalk. I had always wished to see the tarantella danced, and now I had seen it I wished never to see it more. I was so well satisfied that I hastened to drop a few *soldi* into the outstretched tambourine; one of the coins rebounded and fell into the girl's parchment bosom, which would not have made a bad tambourine itself.

My gratuity had the anticipated effect;

the musician took himself off instantly.
But he was only the *avant coureur* of his
detestable tribe.   To dispose at once of this
feature of Neapolitan street life, I will state
that in the course of that morning and afternoon one hundred and seven organ-men
and *zambognari* (bagpipe players) paid
their respects to me.   It is odd, or not, as
you choose to look at it, that the city which
has the eminence of being the first school
of music in the world should be a city of
hand-organs.   I think it explains the constant irritability and the occasional out-
breaks of wrath on the part of Mount Vesuvius.

The youth with strawberries, and his
two companions, the fan-man and the seller
of sea fruit, remained on the curb-stone for
an hour or more, waiting for me to relent.
In most lands, when you inform a trafficker
in nicknacks of your indisposition to purchase his wares, he departs with more or
less philosophy ; but in Naples he some-

times attaches himself to you for the day.
One morning our friend J——, who is
almost morbidly diffident, returned to the
hotel attended by an individual with a guitar, two venders of lava carvings, a leper
in the final stages of decomposition, and
a young lady costumed *en négligé* with a
bunch of violets. J—— had picked up
these charming acquaintances in one of the
principal streets at the remote end of the
town. The perspiration stood nearly an
inch deep on J——'s forehead. He had
vainly done everything to get rid of them :
he had heaped gifts of money on the leper,
bought wildly of cameos and violets, and
even offered to purchase the guitar. But
no ; they clung to him. An American of
this complexion was not caught every day
on the Corso Vittorio Emanuele.

I was so secure from annoyance up there
on my balcony that I did not allow the
three merchants arranged on the curb-stone
to distract me. Occupied with the lively,

many-colored life of the street and the
shore, I failed even to notice when they
went away. Glancing in their direction
somewhat later, I saw that they had gone.
But Masaniello remained, resting the hollow of his back and his two elbows on the
coping of the wall, and becoming a part of
the gracious landscape. He remained there
all day. Why, I shall never know. He
made no demand on my purse, or any over-
ture towards my acquaintance, but stood
there, statuesque, hour after hour, scarcely
changing his attitude — *insouciant*, imper-
turbable, never for an instant relapsing
from that indolent reserve which had
marked him at first, except once, when he
smiled (rather sarcastically, I thought) as
I fell victim to an aged beggar whose band-
aged legs gave me the fancy that they had
died early and been embalmed, and were
only waiting for the rest of the man to die
in order to be buried. Then Masaniello
smiled — at my softness ?   I shall never be
able to explain the man.

Though the Chiatamone is a quiet street for Naples, it would be considered a bustling thoroughfare anywhere else. As the morning wore on, I found entertainment enough in the constantly increasing stream of foot-passengers — soldiers, sailors, monks, peddlers, paupers, and donkeys. Now and then a couple of acrobats in soiled tights and tarnished spangles would spread out their square of carpet in front of the hotel, and go through some innocent feats; or it was a juggler who came along with a sword trick, or a man with *fantoccini,* among which Signor Punchinello was a prominent character, as he invariably is in Italian puppet-shows. This, with the soft Neapolitan laugh and chatter, the cry of orange-girls, the braying of donkeys, and the strident strain of the hand-organ, which interposed itself ever and anon, like a Greek chorus, was doing very well for a quiet little street of no pretensions whatever.

For a din to test the tympanum of your

ear, and a restless swarming of life to turn you dizzy, you should go to the Strada Santa Lucia of a pleasant morning. The houses in this quarter of the city are narrow and tall, many of them seven or eight stories high, and packed like bee-hives, which they further resemble in point of gloominess and stickiness. Here the lower classes live, and if they live chiefly on the sidewalks it is not to be wondered at. In front of the dingy door-ways and arches the women make their soups and their toilets with equal *naïveté* of disregard to passing criticism. The baby is washed, dressed, nursed, and put to sleep, and all the domestic duties performed, *al fresco*. Glancing up the sunny street at some particularly fretful moment of the day, you may chance to catch an instantaneous glimpse of the whole neighborhood spanking its child.

In the Strada Santa Lucia the clattering donkey cart has solved the problem of perpetual motion. Not less noisy and crowded

are those contiguous hill-side lanes and al-
leys (*gradoni*) where you go up and down
stone steps, and can almost touch the buildings on both sides. No wheeled vehicle
ever makes its way here, though sometimes
a donkey, with panniers stuffed full of veg-
etables, may be seen gravely mounting or
descending the slippery staircase, directed
by the yells and ingenious blasphemies of
his driver, who is always assisted in this
matter by sympathetic compatriots standing in door-ways, or leaning perilously out
of seventh story windows. Some of the
streets in this section are entirely given
over to the manufacture of macaroni. On
interminable clothes-lines, stretched along
the sidewalks at the height of a man's head,
the flabby threads of paste are hung to dry,
forming a continuous sheet, which sways
like heavy satin drapery and nearly trails
on the ground; but the dogs run in and out
through the dripping fringe without the
least inconvenience to themselves. Now

and then one will thoughtfully turn back
and lap it. Macaroni was formerly a favorite *plat* of mine. Day and night the
hum of human voices rises from these
shabby streets. As to the smells which in-
fest them — "Give me an ounce of civet,
good apothecary, to sweeten my imagination." Here Squalor reigns, seated on his
throne of mud. But it is happy squalor.
In Naples misery laughs and sings, and
plays the Pandean pipe, and enjoys itself.
Poverty gayly throws its bit of rag over
the left shoulder, and does not seem to perceive the difference between that and a
cloak of Genoese velvet. Neither the cruel
past nor the fateful present has crushed the
joyousness out of Naples. It is the very
Mark Tapley of cities — and that, perhaps,
is what makes it the most pathetic. But
to get back to our balcony.

I am told that the lower classes — always excepting the sixty or seventy thousand *lazzaroni*, who have ceased to exist as

a body, but continue, as individuals, very
effectively to prey upon the stranger — are
remarkable for their frugal and industrious
habits. I suppose this is so, though the
visible results which elsewhere usually follow the thriftiness of a population are ab-
sent from Naples. However, my personal
observation of the workingman was limited
to watching some masons employed on
a building in process of erection a little
higher up on the opposite side of the
strada. I was first attracted by the fact
that the men were planning the blocks of
fawn - colored stone, and readily shaping
them with knives, as if the stone had been
cheese or soap. It was, in effect, a kind of
calcareous tufa, which is soft when newly
quarried, and gradually hardens on expo-
sure. It was not a difficult material to work
in, but the masons set to the task with that
deliberate care not to strain themselves
which I had admired in the horny-handed
laboring man in various parts of Italy. At

intervals of two or three minutes the stone-cutters — there were seven of them — would suddenly suspend operations, and without any visible cause fall into a violent dispute. It looked as if they were coming to blows; but they were only engaged in amicable gossip. Perhaps it was a question of the weather, or of the price of macaroni, or of that heartless trick which Cattarina played upon poor Giuseppe night before last. There was something very cheerful in their chatter, of which I caught only the eye-flashes and the vivacious southern gestures that accompanied it. It was pleasant to see them standing there with crossed legs, in the midst of their honorable toil, leisurely indulging in graceful banter at Heaven only knows how many francs per day. At about half past ten o'clock they abruptly knocked off work altogether (I knew it was coming to that), and, stretching themselves out comfortably under an adjacent shed, went to sleep. Pres-

ently a person — presumably the foreman
— appeared on the scene, and proceeded
energetically to kick the seven sleepers,
who arose and returned to their tools. After straightening out this matter the foreman departed, and the masons, dropping
saw, chisel, and fore-plane, crawled in under the shed again. I smiled, and a glow
came over me as I reflected that perhaps
I had discovered the identical branch of
the Latin race from which the American
plumber has descended to us.

There is one class, forming a very large
portion of the seedy population of Naples,
and the most estimable portion, to whose
industry, integrity, and intelligence I can
unreservedly testify. This class, which, so
far as I saw, does all the hard work that is
done and receives nothing but persecution
in return, is to be met everywhere in Italy,
but nowhere in so great force as in Naples.
I mean those patient, wise little donkeys,
which are as barbarously used by their

masters as ever their masters were by the
Bourbons. In witnessing the senseless cru-
elty with which a Neapolitan treats his inarticulate superior, one is almost disposed
to condone the outrages of Spanish rule.
I have frequently seen a fellow beat one of
the poor animals with a club nearly as
large round as the little creature's body.
As a donkey is generally its owner's sole
source of income, it seems a rather near-
sighted policy to knock the breath out of it.
But, mercifully, the wind is tempered to the
shorn lamb, and the donkey is pachyderma-
tous. A blow that would kill a horse likely
enough merely impresses a donkey with
the idea that somebody is going to hit him.
Under the old order of things in Naples his
insensibility was sometimes outflanked by
removing a strip of his hide, thus laying
bare a responsive spot for the whip-lash;
but that stratagem is now prohibited by
law, I believe. A donkey with a particularly sensitive place on him anywhere naturally fetches a high price at present.

The disproportionate burdens which are imposed upon and stoically accepted by the Neapolitan donkey constantly excite one's wonder and pity. As I sat there on the balcony a tiny cart went by so piled with furniture that the pigmy which drew it was entirely hidden from sight. The cumbersome mass had the appearance of being propelled by some piece of internal machinery. This was followed by another cart, containing the family, I suppose — five or six stupid persons drawn by a creature no larger than a St. Bernard dog. I fell into a train of serious reflection on donkeys in general, chiefly suggested, I rather fancy, by Masaniello, who was still standing with his back against the sea-wall and his eyes fixed on my balcony as I went in to lunch.

II.

WHEN I returned to my post of observation, half an hour later, I found the street nearly deserted. Naples was taking its siesta. A fierce, hot light quivered on the bay and beat down on the silent villas along shore, making the mellow-tinted pilasters and porticoes gleam like snow against the dull green of the olive-trees. The two cones of Mount Vesuvius, now wrapped in a transparent violet haze, which brought them strangely near, had for background a fathomless sky of unclouded azure. Here and there, upon a hill-side in the distance, small white houses, with verandas and balconies

"Close latticed to the brooding heat,"

seemed scorching among their dusty vines. The reflection of the water was almost intolerable.

As I reached up to lower the awning overhead, I had a clairvoyant consciousness that some one was watching me from below. Whether Masaniello had brought his noonday meal of roasted chestnuts with him, or, during my absence, had stolen to some low *trattoria* in the vicinity to refresh himself, I could not tell; but there he was, in the act now of lighting one of those long pipe-stem cigars called Garibaldis.

Since he wanted neither my purse nor my person, what was his design in hanging about the hotel? Perhaps it *was* my person he wanted; perhaps he was an emissary of the police; but no, the lowest government official in Italy always wears enough gold-lace for a Yankee major-general. Besides, I was innocent; I had n't done it, whatever it was. Possibly Masaniello mistook me for somebody else, and was meditating a neat stiletto stroke or two if I ventured out after night-fall. Indeed, I intended to go to the theatre of San Carlo that night. A rush —

a flash of steel in the moonlight, an echoing foot-fall — and all would be over before one could explain anything. Masaniello was becoming monotonous.

I turned away from him to look at the Castel dell' Ovo, within rifle range at my left, on a small island connected by an arched breakwater with the main-land at the foot of the Pizzofalcone. I tried to take in the fact that this wrinkled pile was begun by William I. in 1154, and completed a century later by Frederick II.; that here, in the reign of Robert the Wise, came the witty Giotto to decorate the chapel with those frescoes of which only the tradition remains; that here Charles III. of Durazzo held Queen Joanna a prisoner, and was here besieged by Louis of Anjou; that, finally, in 1495, Charles VIII. of France knocked over the old castle, and Pedro de Toledo set it up on its legs again in 1532. I tried, but rather unsuccessfully, to take in all this, for though the castle boasts of bastions and outworks, it lacks the heroic aspect. In fact, it is now used as a prison, and has the right hang-dog look of prisons. However, I put my fancy to work restoring the castle to the strength and dignity it wore in chronicler Froissart's day, and was about to attack the place with the assistance of the aforesaid Charles VIII., when the heavy tramp of feet and the measured tap of a drum chimed in very prettily with my hostile intention. A regiment of infantry was coming down the strada.

If I do not describe this regiment as the very poorest regiment in the world, it is because it was precisely like every other body of Italian soldiery that I have seen. The men were small, spindle-legged, and slouchy. One might have taken them for raw recruits if their badly-fitting white-duck uniforms had not shown signs of veteran service. As they wheeled into the Chiatamone, each man trudging along at

his own gait, they looked like a flock of
sheep. The bobbing mass recalled to my
mind — by that law of contraries which
makes one thing suggest another totally
different — the compact, grand swing of the
New York Seventh Regiment as it swept
up Broadway the morning it returned from
Pennsylvania at the close of the draft riots
in '63. If the National Guard had shuffled
by in the loose Garibaldian fashion, I do
not believe New York would have slept
with so keen a sense of security as it did
that July night.

The room directly under mine was occupied by a young English lady, who, attracted by the roll of the drums, stepped
out on her balcony just as the head of the
column reached the hotel. In her innocent
desire to witness a military display she
probably had no anticipation of the tender
fusillade she would have to undergo. That
the colonel should give the fair stranger a
half-furtive salute, in which he cut nothing

in two with his sabre, was well enough;
but that was no reason why every mother's
son in each platoon should look up at the
balcony as he passed, and then turn and
glance back at her over his musket. Yet
this singular military evolution, which I
cannot find set down anywhere in Hardee's
Tactics, was performed by every man in
the regiment. That these ten or twelve
hundred warriors refrained from kissing
their hands to the blonde lady shows the
severe discipline which prevails in the Italian army. Possibly there was not a man of
them, from the colonel's *valet* down to the
colonel himself, who did not march off with
the conviction that he had pierced that
blue muslin wrapper somewhere in the region of the left breast. I must relate that
the modest young Englishwoman stood this
enfilading fire admirably, though it made
white and red roses of her complexion.

The rear of the column was brought up,
and emphasized, if I may say it, by an ex-

clamation point in the shape of a personage
so richly gilded and of such gorgeous plu-
mage that I should instantly have accepted
him as the King of Italy if I had not long
ago discovered that fine feathers do not always make fine birds. It was only the reg-
imental physician. Of course he tossed up
a couple of pill-like eyes to the balcony as
he strutted by, with his plume standing out
horizontally — like that thin line of black
smoke which just then caught my attention
in the offing.

This was the smoke from the pipe of
the funny little steamer which runs from
Naples to Sorrento, and thence to Capri,
where it drops anchor for so brief a space
that you are obliged to choose between a
scramble up the rocks to the villa of Tiberius and a visit in a small boat to the Blue
Grotto, that "sapphire shell of the Siren of
Naples," as Quinet neatly calls it. The
steamer is supposed to leave the Chiaia at
Naples every morning at a stated hour;

but you need not set your heart on going
to Capri by that steamer on any particular
day. It goes or not just as the captain happens to feel about it when the time comes.
A cinder in his eye, a cold in his head, a
conjugal tiff over his *polenta* — in fine, any
insignificant thing is apparently sufficient
to cause him to give up the trip. It is only
moderate satisfaction you get out of him on
these occasions. He throws his arms de-
spairingly in the air, and making forked
lightning with his fingers cries, " Ah, mercy of God! no — we sail not this day! "
Then wildly beating his forehead with his
knuckles, " To-morrow, yes! " There is
ever a pleasing repose of manner in an ex-
cited Italian.

I suspect the truth is that some of the
directors of the steamboat company are mediæval saints, and that the anniversaries of
their birthdays or their deathdays interfere
with business. The captain is an excellent
fellow of his sort, and extremely devout,

though that does not prevent him from now and then playing a very scurvy trick upon his passengers. Of course one's main object in going to Capri is to see the Blue Grotto, the entrance to which is through a small arch scarcely three feet high in the face of the rock. With the sea perfectly tranquil, you are obliged to bow your head or lie down in the wherry while passing in; but with a north or west wind breathing, it is impossible to enter at all. When this chances to be the case the captain is careful not to allude to the matter, but smilingly allows you to walk aboard, and pitilessly takes you out under a scorching sky to certain disappointment and a clam-bake, in which you perform the rôle of the clam.

Through my glass I could see the little egg-shell of a steamer, which for some reason had come to a stop in the middle of the bay, with a thread of smoke issuing from her funnel and embroidering itself in fanciful patterns on the sunny atmosphere. I knew how hot it was over there, and I knew that the light westerly breeze which crisped the water and became a suffocating breath before it reached shore had sealed up the Grotta Azzurra for that day. I pictured the pleasure-seekers scattered about the heated deck, each dejectedly munching his Dead Sea apple of disappointment. The steamer was evidently getting under way again, for the thread of smoke had swollen into a black, knotted cable. Presently a faint whistle came across the water — as if a ghost were whistling somewhere in the distance — and the vessel went puffing away towards Castellamare. If the Emperor Tiberius Claudius Nero Cæsar could have looked down just then from the cloudy battlements of Capri, what would he have thought of that!

The great squares of shadow cast upon the street by the hotel and the adjoining buildings were deepening by degrees. Fitful puffs of air came up from the bay — the early precursors of that refreshing breeze which the Mediterranean sends to make the summer twilights of Naples delicious. Now and then a perfume was wafted to the balcony, as if the wind had stolen a handful of scents from some high-walled inclosure of orange-trees and acacias, and flung it at me. The white villas, set in their mosaic of vines on the distant hill-side, had a cooler look than they wore earlier in the day. The heat was now no longer oppressive, but it made one drowsy — that and the sea air: An hour or more slipped away from me unawares. Meanwhile, the tide of existence had risen so imperceptibly at my feet that I was surprised, on looking down, suddenly to find the strada flooded with streams of carriages and horsemen and pedestrians. All the gay life of Naples, that had lain dormant through the heavy noon, had awakened, like the princess in the enchanted palace, to take up the laugh where it left off and order fresh ices at the cafés.

I had a feeling that Masaniello — he was still there — was somehow at the bottom of all this; that by some *diablerie* of his, may be with the narcotic fumes of that black cigar, he had thrown the city into the lethargy from which it was now recovering.

The crowd, which flowed in two opposing currents past the hotel, was a gayer and more smartly dressed throng than that of the morning. Certain shabby aspects, however, were not wanting, for donkey carts mingled themselves jauntily with the more haughty equipages on their way to the Riviera di Chiaia, the popular drive. There were beautiful brown women, with heavy-fringed eyes, in these carriages, and now and then a Neapolitan dandy — a creature *sui generis* — rode along-side on horseback. Every human thing that can scrape a vehicle together goes to the Riviera di Chiaia of a fine afternoon. It is a magnificent wide avenue, open on one side to the bay, and lined on the other with palaces and villas and hotels. The road leads to the Grotto of Posilippo, and to endless marvels beyond — the tomb of Virgil, Lake Avernus, Baiæ, Cumæ, a Hellenic region among whose ruins wander the sorrowful shades of the gods. But the afternoon idler is not likely to get so far; after a turn or two on the promenade, he is content to sit under the trees in the garden of the Villa Nazionale, sipping his sherbet dashed with snow, and listening to the band.

I saw more monks this day than I met in a week at Rome, their natural headquarters; but in Naples, as in the Eternal City, they are generally not partial to busy thoroughfares. I think some religious festival must have been going on in a church near the Chiatamone. A solemn, dark-robed figure gliding in and out among the merry crowd had a queer, pictorial effect, and gave me an incongruous twelfth-century sort of sensation. Once a file of monks — I do not remember ever seeing so many together outside a convent — passed swiftly under the balcony. I was near tumbling into the Middle Ages, when their tonsured heads reminded me of that row of venerable elderly gentlemen one always sees in the front orchestra chairs at the ballet, and I was thus happily dragged back into my own cycle.

It was a noisy, light-hearted, holiday people that streamed through the strada in the waning sunshine; they required no policeman, as a similar crowd in England or America would have done; their merriment was as harmless as that of so many birds, though no doubt there was in these laughing throngs plenty of the dangerous stuff out of which graceful brigands and picturesque assassins are made. But it was easier and pleasanter to discover here and there a face or a form such as the old masters loved to paint. I amused myself in selecting models for new pictures by Titian and Raphael and Carlo Dolci and Domenichino, to take the places of those madonnas and long-tressed mistresses of which nothing will remain in a few centuries. What will Italy be when she has lost her masterpieces, as she has lost the art that produced them ? To-day she is the land of paintings, without any painters, the empty cradle of poets.

I do not know that anything in the lively street entertained me more than the drivers of the public carriages. Like all the common Neapolitans, the Jehus have a wonderful gift of telegraphing with their fingers. It is not a question of words laboriously spelled out, but of a detailed statement in a flash. They seem to be able to do half an hour's talking in a couple of seconds. A fillip of the finger-joint, and there's a sentence for you as long as one of Mr. Carlyle's. At least, that is my idea of it ; it is merely conjecture on my part, for though I have frequently formed the topic of a conversation carried on in this style under my very nose, I never succeeded in overhearing anything. I have undoubtedly been anathematized, and barely probable, been complimented; but in those instances, like Horatio, I took fortune's buffets and rewards with equal thanks. It is diverting to see two of these fellows meeting at a breakneck pace and exchanging verdicts on their respective passengers. May be one, with a gesture like lightning, says: "I've a rich English milor; he has n't asked for my tariff; I shall bleed him beautifully, *per Bacco!*" At the same instant the other possibly hurls back: "No such luck! A pair of foolish Americani, but they 've a pig of a courier who pockets all the *buonamano* himself, the devil fly away with him!" Thus they meet, and indulge in their simple prattle, and are out of each other's sight, all in the twinkling of an eye.

III.

THE twilights in Southern Italy fall suddenly, and are of brief duration. While I was watching the darkening shadow of the hotel on the opposite sea-wall, the dusk closed in, and the street began rapidly to empty itself. A curtain of mist was already stretched from headland to headland, shutting out the distant objects. Here and there on a jutting point a light blossomed, its duplicate glassed in the water, as if the fiery flower had dropped a petal. Presently there were a hundred lights, and then a thousand, fringing the crescented shore.

On our leaving Rome, the landlord had pathetically warned us of the fatal effects of the night air in Naples, just as our Neapolitan host, at a later date, let fall some disagreeable hints about the Roman malaria. They both were right. In this delicious land Death shrouds himself in the dew and lurks in all gentle things. The breeze from the bay had a sudden chill in it now; the dampness of the atmosphere was as heavy as a fine rain. I pushed back my chair on the balcony, and then I lingered a moment to see the moon rising over Capri. Then I saw how that bay, with its dreadful mountain, was lovelier than anything on earth. I turned from it reluctantly, and as I glanced into the silent street beneath, there was Masaniello, a black silhouette against the silvery moonlight.

VII.

SMITH.

VII.

SMITH.

AN old acquaintance of mine, who has gone away into the dark with all his mirthful sayings, once described an English servant as " the valet of the Shadow of Death." The *mot* was said not to be original with my friend, but I have heard so many brilliant things from those same lips that I do not care to go further in search of an owner for what is sufficiently characteristic of him to be his. Whoever first said it gave us in a single phrase the most perfect *croquis* that ever was made of the English servingman. We all know him in the English novel of the period, and some of us know him in the flesh. I chance myself to be familiar with a mild form of him. I speak of him as if he were a disease : in his most aggravated type I should say he might be considered as an affliction. Thackeray — the satirist and biographer, the Pope and Plutarch, of Jeemes — frankly admitted he was afraid of the creature. That kindly keen blue eye, which saw through the shams and follies of Mayfair, was wont to droop under the stony stare of his host's butler. I hasten to confess to only a limited personal knowledge of the august being in plush small-clothes and pink silk stockings who presides over the grand houses in England, for I carried my pilgrim's wallet into few grand houses there ; but I have had more or less to do with certain humble brothers of his, who are leading lives of highly respectable gloom in sundry English taverns and hotels.

It is one of these less dazzling brothers who furnishes me with the *motif* of this brief study. More fortunate than that Roman emperor who vainly longed to have all his enemies consolidated into a single neck,

I have secured in a person named Smith the epitome of an entire class — not, indeed, with the cruel intent of dispatching him, but of photographing him. I should decline to take Smith's head by any less gentle method.

In London there is a kind of hotel of which we have no counterpart in the United States. This hotel is usually located in some semi-aristocratic side street, and wears no badge of its servitude beyond a large, well-kept brass door-plate, bearing the legend "Jones's Hotel" or "Brown's Hotel," as the case may be; but be it Brown or Jones, he has been dead at least fifty years, and the establishment is conducted by Robinson. There is no coffee-room or public dining-room, or even office, in this hotel; the commercial traveller is an unknown quantity there; your meals are served in your apartments; the furniture is solid and comfortable, the attendance admirable, the *cuisine* unexceptionable, and the bill abominable. But for ease, quietness, and a sort of 1812 odor of respectability, this hotel has nothing to compare with it in the wide world. It is here that the intermittent homesickness you contracted on the Continent will be lifted out of your bosom; it is here will be unfolded to you alluring vistas of the substantial comforts that surround the private lives of prosperous Britons; it is here, above all, that you will be brought in contact with Smith.

It was on our arrival in London, one April afternoon, that the door of what looked like a private mansion, in D—— Street, was thrown open to us by a boy broken out all over with buttons. Behind this boy stood Smith. I call him simply Smith for two reasons: in the first place because it is convenient to do so, and in the second place because that is what he called himself. I wish it were as facile a matter to explain how this seemingly unobtrusive person instantly took possession of us, bullied us with his usefulness, and knocked us down with his urbanity. From the moment he stepped forward to relieve us of our hand-luggage, we were his — and remained his until that other moment, some weeks later, when he handed us our parcels again, and stood statuesque on the doorstep, with one finger lifted to his forehead in decorous salute, as we drove away. Ah, what soft despotism was that which was exercised for no other end than to anticipate our requirements — to invent new wants for us only to satisfy them! If I anywhere speak lightly of Smith, if I take exception to his preternatural gravity (of which I would not have him moult a feather), if I allude invidiously to his lifelong struggle with certain rebellious letters of the alphabet, it is out of sheer envy and regret that we have nothing like him in America. We have Niagara, and the Yosemite, and Edison's Electric Light (or shall have it, when we get it), but we have no trained serving-men like Smith. He is the result of older and vastly more complex social conditions than ours. His training began in the feudal ages. An atmosphere charged with machicolated battlements and cathedral spires was necessary to his perfect development, — that, and generation after generation of lords and princes and wealthy country-gentlemen for him to practice on. He is not possible in New England. The very cut of his features is unknown among us. It has been remarked that each trade and profession has its physiognomy, its own proper face. If you look closely you will detect a family likeness running through the portraits of Garrick and Kean and Booth and Irving. There's the self-same sabre-like flash in the eye of Marlborough and Bonaparte — the same resolute labial expression. Every lackey in London might be the son or brother of any other lackey. Smith's father, and his

father's father, and so on back to the gray
dawn of England, were serving-men, and
each in turn has been stamped with the im-
mutable trade-mark of his class. Waiters
(like poets) are born, not made; and they
have not had time to be born in America.

As a shell that has the care of inclosing
a pearl like Smith, Jones's Hotel demands
a word or two of more particular description. The narrow little street in which it
is situated branches off from a turbulent
thoroughfare, and is quite packed with historical, social, and literary traditions. Here,
at the close of his days, dwelt the learned
and sweet-minded philosopher, John Evelyn, the contemporary and friend of everybody's friend, Mr. Samuel Pepys, of the
admiralty. I like to think of Evelyn turning out of busy Piccadilly into this more
quiet precinct, accompanied, perhaps, by
the obsequious Samuel himself. According
to Jesse, the witty Dr. Arburthnot also resided here, after the death of his royal pa-

troness, Queen Anne, had driven him from his snug quarters in St. James's Palace. Hither came Pope, Swift, Gray, Parnell, Prior, and a flock of other singing-birds and brilliant wits to visit the worthy doctor. As I sit of an evening in our parlor, which is on a level with the sidewalk, the ghostly echo of those long-silent footfalls is more distinct to my ear than the tread of the living passers-by. The earthly abiding places of obsolete notabilities are very thick in this neighborhood. A few minutes' walk takes you to the ugly walled mansion that once held the beauty, but could not hold all the radiance, of Georgiana Duchess of Devonshire, and a little further on is Apsley House.

But we need not wander. D—— Street still has high pretensions of its own. I take it that several families whose consequence is to be found in Debrett's Peerage have their town-houses here. Over the sculptured door-way of a sombre edifice

which sets somewhat back behind a tower-
ing iron *grille* with gilded spear-heads, I
have noticed a recently hung hatchment —
an intimation that death is no respecter of
English nobility. At the curb-stone of a
spacious, much-curtained mansion directly
opposite the hotel, there is a constant arrival and departure of broughams and lan-
daus, with armorial blazons and powdered
footmen. From these carriages descend
bewitching slips of English maidenhood
with peach-bloom complexions, and richly-
dressed, portly dowagers shod with perfectly flat-soled shoes. But I confess that
the periodical rattling by of a little glazed
cart lettered " Scarlet the Butcher " inter-
ests me more ; for no mortal reason, I suppose, except that Scarlet seems a phenom-
enally appropriate name for a gentleman
in his line of business.

I am afraid my description of Jones's
Hotel is very like one of those old Spanish
comedies,

> "In which you see,
> As Lope says, the history of the world,
> Brought down from Genesis to the Day of Judgment."

The building itself, arguing from the thickness of the walls and the antiquated style of the interior wood-work, must have stood its ground a great many years. I do not know how long it has been a hotel; perhaps for the better part of a century. In the first instance it was doubtless the home of some titled family. I indulge the fancy that there was a lot of lovely, high-bred daughters, who drew gay company here. The large, lofty-studded rooms were meant for an opulent, hospitable kind of life to inhabit them. Opening on the wide hall — where Buttons is always sitting, a perfect young Cerberus, waiting for the door-bell to ring — is a small dressing-cabinet, in which, I make no question, his lordship has many a time sworn like a pirate over the extravagance of the girls. I know he has discharged the butler there. A fitful, evasive odor, as of faded rose-leaves in a forgotten drawer, seems to linger in these chambers, and I think there are hints in the air of old-time laughter and of sobs that have long since hushed themselves into silence. The parlor is full of suggestions to me, especially at twilight, before the candles are brought in. Sometimes I can almost hear a muffled, agitated voice murmuring out of the Past, "Leave me, Bellamore!" and I have an impression that he did n't leave her. How could he, with those neat diamond buckles glistening at her instep, and her pretty brown hair frosted with silver powder, and that distracting dot of court-plaster stuck near the left corner of her rosy mouth! The old walls are very discreet, not to say incommunicative, on this subject; it is not for them to betray the joys and sorrows and sins of yesterday, and I have to evolve these matters out of my own synthetic imagination. But I am certain that Bellamore did n't leave her!

Overhead there are suites of apartments identical with our own, and I believe they are occupied — by serious-minded families of phantoms; they come and go so softly. There is no loud talking on the staircase, no slamming of doors, no levity of any description among the inmates of this hostelry. Whoever comes here finds his nature subdued to the color of his surroundings, like the dyer's hand. The wildest guest shortly succumbs to the soothing influence of Smith. He pervades the place like an atmosphere, and fits it so perfectly that, without jarring on the present, he seems a figure projected out of that dusky past which has lured me too long, and will catch me again before we get through.

Smith is a man of about forty, but so unassuming that I do not think he would assume to be so old or so young as that: tall and straight, with scant, faded brown hair parted in the middle, and a deferential cough; clammy blue eyes, thin lips, a sed-

entary complexion, and careful side-whis-
kers. He is always in evening dress, and
wears white cotton gloves, which set your
teeth on edge, during dinner service. He
is a person whose gravity of deportment is
such as to lend seriousness to the coal-scut-
tle when he replenishes the parlor fire — a
ceremony which the English April makes
imperative, the English April being as raw
as an American February.

Smith's respect for you, at least its outward manifestation, is accompanied by a
deep, unexpressed respect for himself. He
not only knows his own place, but he
knows yours, and holds you to it. He is
incapable of venturing on a familiarity, or
of submitting to one. He can wrap up
more pitying disapprobation in a scarcely
perceptible curl of his nether lip than another man could express in a torrent of
words. I have gone about London a whole
forenoon with one of Smith's thin smiles
clinging like a blister to my consciousness.

12

He is not taciturn, but he gives you the impression of unconquerable reserve. Though he seldom speaks, except to answer an inquiry, he has managed in some occult fashion to permeate us with a knowledge of his domestic environment. For the soul of me, I cannot say how I came by the information that Smith married Lady Hadelaide Scarborough's first maid twelve years ago, nor in what manner I got hold of the idea that Lady Hadelaide Scarborough's first maid rather stooped from her social status when she formed a matrimonial alliance with him. Yet these facts are undeniably in my possession. I also understand that Smith regards Mrs. Smith — who quitted service at the time of this *mésalliance* — as a sort of fragment (a little finger-joint, if that will help convey my meaning) of Lady Hadelaide herself. There's an air of very good society about Smith. He evidently has connecting tendrils with beings who, if they are not roses themselves, have the privilege of constituting the dust at the roses' feet. If Smith were to make any statement to me concerning the movements of Royalty, I should believe him. If he were to confide to me that Her Majesty, accompanied by the Princess Beatrice, walked for a few seconds yesterday afternoon on the terrace at Windsor, I should know it was so, even if I failed to see the event recorded in The Times.

Smith has been very near to Royalty. To be sure, it was fallen royalty, so I shall waste no capital letters on it. It fell at Sedan, and picked itself up in a manner, and came over to London, where Smith had the bliss of waiting upon it. " The Hemperor was a very civil-spoken gentleman," observed Smith, detailing the circumstances with an air of respectful patronage, and showing that he had a nice sense of the difference between an English sovereign and an uncurrent Napoleon.

The plain truth is that Smith is an arrant gossip about himself without in the least having the appearance of it. He so ingeniously embroiders bits of his autobiography on alien textures that one is apt to get a detail or two quite unawares. I do not know how or when six little Smiths glided into my intelligence (they cost me a shilling a head), but I think it was in connection with an inquiry on my part as to what hour the morning train left Paddington Station for Stratford-upon-Avon. Two nights out of the week Smith retires to his domestic domicile; situated, I infer, in some remote suburb of London, for he always takes a bag with him — a respectable, drab-colored hand-bag, with a monogram on it. At a little distance the twisted initials, in raised worsted, resemble a reduced copy of the Laocoön, the prominent serpentine S having, I suspect, no small share in producing that effect. I somehow pose and mix up the six little Smiths in this monogram.

I have said that Smith took possession of our party immediately on its arrival at Jones's Hotel, but we were not at once conscious of the fact. We had arrived there in high spirits, glad to have left a tedious sea-voyage behind us, and rejoiced to find ourselves in London — the London we had dreamed of these ten or twenty years. But presently we felt there was something in the temperature that chilled our vivacity. We were a thousand miles from suspecting what it was. Our purpose in London was to see the sights, to visit all those historic buildings and monuments and galleries which were wrested from us by the war of 1776. Our wanderings through the day were often long and always fatiguing; we returned jaded to the hotel, frequently after the dinner hour, and in no mood to undertake radical changes in our costume. There stood Smith in his crisp neck-tie and claw-hammer coat and immaculate gloves. The dinner was elegant in its appointments, and exquisitely served. The dressing of the salad was rivalled only by the dressing of Smith. Yet something was wrong. We were somehow repressed, and for three days we did not know what it was that repressed us. On the fourth day I resolved to give our party a little surprise by appearing at dinner in conventional broadcloth and white breastplate. Each of the other two members of the coterie — insensibly under the magnetism of Smith — had planned a like surprise. When we met at table and surveyed each other, we laughed aloud — for the first time in three days in Smith's presence. It was plain to see that Smith approved of an elaborate dinner toilette, and henceforth we adopted it.

Presently we were struck, and then began to be appalled, by the accuracy, minuteness, and comprehensiveness of Smith's knowledge of London. It was encyclopædic. He was a vitalized time-table of railways and coaches and steamboats, a walk-

ing, breathing directory to all the shops,
parks, churches, museums, and theatres of
the bewildering Babylon. He had, stamped
on his brain, a map of all the tangled omni-
bus routes ; he knew the best seats in every
place of amusement, the exact moment the
performance began in each, and could put
his finger without hesitating a second on
the very virtuoso's collection you wanted
to examine. This is not the half of his ac-
complishments. I despair of stating them.
I do not see how he ever had the leisure to
collect such a mass of detail. It seems to
substantiate a theory I have that Smith
has existed, with periodic renewals of his
superficial structure, from the time of the
Norman Conquest. Before we discovered
his almost wicked amplitude of information, we used to consult him touching intended pilgrimages, but shortly gave it up,
finding that our provincial plans generally
fell cold upon him. He was almost amused,
one day, at our desire to ascertain the

whereabouts of that insignificant house in Cheapside — it is No. 17, if I remember — in which Keats wrote his sonnet on Chapman's Homer. Our New World curiosity as to certain localities which possess no interest whatever to the Londoner must often have struck Smith as puerile. His protest or his disapproval — I do not know how to name it — was always so evanescent and shadowy that he cannot be said to have expressed it; it was something in his manner, and not in his words, — something as vague as a fleeting breath on a window-glass; but it dampened us.

There is a singular puissance in a grave, chilling demeanor, though it may be backed by no solid quality whatever. Nothing so imposes on the world. I have known persons to attain very high social and public distinction by no other means than a guarded solemnity of manner. Even when we see through its shallowness, we are still impressed by it, just as children are para-

lyzed by a sheeted comrade, though they
know all the while it is only one of themselves playing ghost.

I suppose it was in the course of nature
that we should have fallen under the dom-
ination of Smith, and have come to accept
him with a degree of seriousness which
seems rather abject to me in retrospect.
Without acknowledging it to ourselves, we
were affected by his intangible criticism.
I would not have had it come to his ears
for a five-pound note that I had a habit of
eating a chop in a certain snuffy old coffee-
house near Temple Bar, whenever lunch-
time chanced to catch me in that vicinity.

"O plump head-waiter at The Cock,"

to which I most resorted, I should have
been ashamed to have Smith know that I
had the slightest acquaintance with you,
though Tennyson himself has sung your
praises ! Nor would I have had Smith get
wind of the low-bred excursion I made, one
day, up the Thames, in a squalid steamer

crowded with grimy workingmen and their frouzy wives and their children. I hid in my heart the guilty joy I took in two damaged musicians aboard — a violin and a flageolet. The flageolet — I am speaking of the performer — had such a delightfully disreputable patch over his right eye! By the way, I wonder why it is that vagrant players of wind-instruments in England usually have a patch over one eye. Are they combative as a class, or is it that they now and then blow out a visual organ with too assiduous practice in early youth? The violin-man, on the other hand — perhaps I ought to say on the other leg — was lame. Altogether the pair looked like the remains of a band that had been blown up by a steam-boiler explosion on some previous trip on the river. They played a very doleful tune ; full of unaccountable gruffnesses and shrillnesses, which it was my mood to accept as the ghostly replication of the cries and complaints of their late comrades on the occasion suggested. There was a rough crowd on board, with a sprinkling of small shop-keepers, and here and there a group of gaudily-dressed young women, not to be set down in the category of doubtful characters. These people were off on a holiday, and it was curious to observe the heavy, brutal way they took their pleasure, turning it into a hardship. I got a near view of a phase of English life not to be met with in the rarefied atmosphere of D—— Street, and I regret to admit that I have many a time enjoyed myself less in better company. When I returned to the hotel that night, Smith stood rebukefully drying The Pall Mall Gazette for me before the parlor fire.

A year or two of Smith would make it difficult for a man to dispense with him. With Smith for a valet, one would have no distinct wants to perplex one, for Smith's intuition would head them off and supply them before they were formulated. He was, as I have more than hinted, an invaluable servant. Sometimes, as I have looked at him, and reflected on his unmurmuring acceptance of a life of servitude, and the kind of sober grace he threw about its indignity, I used to call to mind that disgruntled, truculent waiter described by John Hay in his charming Castilian Days. "I know a gentleman in the West," says Mr. Hay, "whose circumstances had forced him to become a waiter in a backwoods restaurant. He bore a deadly grudge at the profession that kept him from starving, and asserted his unconquered nobility of soul by scowling at his customers and swearing at the viands he dispensed. I remember the deep sense of wrong with which he would growl, 'Two buckwheats, be gawd!'"

As to Smith's chronic gloom, it really had nothing of moroseness in it — only an habitual melancholy, a crystallized patience. We doubtless put it to some crucial tests with our American ideas and idioms. The

earlier part of our acquaintanceship was
fraught with mutual perplexities. It was
the longest time before we discovered that
ay ill meant Hay Hill Street, Smith making a single mouthful of it, thus — *ayill*.
One morning he staggered us by asking if
we would like " a hapricot freeze " for des-
sert. We assented, and would have assented if he had proposed iced hippopota-
mus ; but the nature of the dish was a mystery to us, and perhaps never, since the
world took shape out of chaos, was there
a simple mould of apricot jelly looked forward to in such poignant suspense. It is
scarcely permissible in so light a sketch as
this to touch on anything so heavy as phi-
lology ; but I cannot forbear wondering
what malign spirit has bewitched the vow-
els of the lower-class Englishman. When
he finds it impossible to elide the vowel at
the beginning of a word, he invariably cov-
ers it with an *h* — the very letter that
plays the deuce with him under ordinary

circumstances. An Oxford scholar once informed me that this peculiarity was the result of imperfect education, and left me to settle it for myself why the peculiarity was confined to England. Illiterate Americans — if there are any — do not drop their *h*'s. But as I have said, this is too heavy a text.

It seems almost an Irish bull to say that one can be in London only once for the first time. In other places you may renew first impressions. A city on the Continent always remains a foreign city to you, no matter how often you visit it; but that first time in London is an experience which can never be made to repeat itself. Whatever is alien to you fades away under your earliest glances; the place suddenly takes home-like aspects; certain streets and courts where you never set foot before strike you familiarly. It is a place where you might have lived — this great seething metropolis — where perhaps you once did live, in hose and doublet or knightly harness, in some immemorial century. I doubt if an American ever visited England without feeling in his bosom the vibration, more or less distinct, of these invisible threads of attachment. Everywhere in the lucid prose of Hawthorne's English Note-Books and Our Old Home this sentiment lies imbedded, like a spray of fossilized fern.

The architecture, the language, and the customs are yours, or must have been yours long ago. Smith himself dawns upon you as a former acquaintance. Possibly he was one of your retainers in the time of Henry VIII. (You like to picture yourself with retainers; for to be an Englishman, and not a duke or an earl, is to miss four fifths of the good luck.) Your imagination gives you a long lease of existence when you fall into reveries of this nature; you fancy yourself extant at various interesting periods of English history; it costs you no effort, while you are about it, to have a hand in a dozen different reigns. What a

picturesque, highly decorative, household-
art sort of life you may lead from the era
of the Black Prince down to the Victorian
age! How lightly you assume the respon-
sibility of prolonging Smith through all
this! He holds the bridle of an extra
horse for you at Poitiers, and also at that
other bloody field of Agincourt; and then,
somewhat later, sits on the box of your
glass coach (which Mr. Samuel Pepys, sur-
veying it from his chamber window, pro-
nounces "mightily fine") as you drive
through the shrewish winter morning to
the Palace of Whitehall to witness the re-
moval of Charles the First's head.

It is easy to shape any kind of chimera
out of that yellowish London fog. Immediately after this epoch, however, your impressions of having been personally associated with the events of English history
become dimmer, if not altogether confused;
possibly your spirit was about that time
undergoing certain organic changes, neces-

sary to the metempsychosis which befel
you later.

You break from your abstraction to the
consciousness that you are a stranger in
your native land. The *genius loci* does not
recognize you; you are an altered man.
You are an American. Yet a little while
ago the past of England was as much your
past as it is Smith's, or that of any Briton
of them all. But you have altered, and
forfeited it. Smith has not altered: he is
the same tall, efficient serving-man he was
in the time of the Plantagenets. He has
that air of having been carefully handed
down which stamps so many things in
England. (If this has been said before, I
beg somebody's pardon; I am treading on
much-walked-over ground.) There, indeed,
Nature seems careful of the type. The
wretched woman who murders Kathleen
Mavourneen in the street under your window shares this quality of permanency with
Smith. She, or one precisely like her, has

been singing ballads for ages, and will go on doing it. Endless generations of American tourists, lodging temporarily at Jones's perpetual Hotel, will give her inexhaustible shillings, and Smith will carry them out to her on his indestructible waiter. The individual Smith may occasionally die, but not the type, not the essence. My mind can take in Macaulay's picture of the New Zealander sitting on a broken buttress of London Bridge, and cynically contemplating the débris — " a landscape with figure," as the catalogues would put it — but I am unable to grasp the idea of the annihilation of anything so firmly established by precedent as Smith. I fancy that even out of the splintered masonry his respectful, well-modulated chest voice would be heard saying (through sheer force of habit), " Will you 'ave a look at the hevening paper, sir?" or, " If you please, sir, the 'ansom is at the door ! "

VIII.

A DAY IN AFRICA.

VIII.

A DAY IN AFRICA.

I.

I AM not immodest enough to assume to speak for other readers, but for my own part I have become rather tired of African travellers. One always knows beforehand what they have in their pack, and precisely the way in which they will spread out their wares. The victorious struggle with the lion and the hairbreadth escape from death at the hands of the native chiefs are matters easily anticipated; and that romantic young savage who attaches himself body and soul to the person of the adventurer, and invariably returns with him to civilization — what a threadbare figure that is! How well we know him under his various guttural aliases! Yet what would six months in Africa amount to without this lineal descendant of Robinson Crusoe's man Friday?

I may seem to display a want of tact in disparaging African travellers, being, in a humble fashion, an African traveller myself, but I have a rare advantage over everybody who has ever visited that country, and written about it — I remained there only one day. The standpoint from which I view the Dark Continent is thus unique. If I had remained a year, or even a fortnight, I should have ceased to be original. I should naturally have killed my lion, tempted the appetite of the anthropophagite, and brought home a little negro boy. I did none of these things, and instead of obscurely falling in at the tail end of a long line of African explorers, I claim to stand quite alone, and in an attitude so wholly unconventional as to entitle it to copyright. So far as I am aware, the idea never before entered the head of any man to travel five thousand miles to Africa, and then to stay there only twenty-four hours !

I must admit, however, that this idea did not take quite that definite form in my mind in the first instance. A visit to Tangier was not down in my itinerary at all, but on reaching Gibraltar, after prolonged wandering through the interior of Spain, Africa threw itself in my way, so to speak. There, just across the narrow straits, lay the tawny barbaric shore. Standing at an embrasure of one of those marvellous sub-terranean batteries which render Gibraltar impregnable — long galleries tunnelled in the solid rock, and winding up to the very summit of the vast pile — I almost fancied I could make out the lion-colored line of the Barbary coast. A magical sea-haze that morning, together with a strip of dun cloud lying low against the horizon, encouraged the illusion. It was purely an illusion, for it is three good hours and a half by steamer from the boat-landing at the foot of Waterport Street to the dismantled, God-forsaken mole at Tangier.

II.

I DO not believe there is a dirtier little
steamer in the world than the one that
plies between Gibraltar and Morocco, and
I am positive that since Noah's ark no vessel ever put to sea with a more variegated
and incongruous lot of passengers than saluted my eyes as I stepped on board the
Jackal one April afternoon. The instant
I set foot on deck I had passed out of Europe. Here were the squalor and the glit-
ter of the Orient — the solemn dusky faces
that look out on the reader from the pages
of the Arabian Nights, and the thousand
and one disagreeable odors of which that
fascinating chronicle makes no mention.
Such a chattering in Spanish, Portuguese,
Hebrew, and Arabic! Such queer brown-
legged figures in pointed hoods and yellow
slippers! Though there were first and sec-

ond class fares, there appeared to be no distinction in the matter of accommodation. From stem to stern the long narrow deck was crowded with Moors, Arabs, negroes, Jews, and half-breeds, inextricably mixing themselves up with empty fruit crates, bamboo baskets, and bales of merchandise. I speculated as to what would become of all that loose luggage if we were to encounter a blow outside; for this placid-looking summer sea has a way of lashing itself into an ungovernable rage without any perceptible provocation. In case of wet weather there was no shelter except a stifling cabin between-decks, where the thirsty were waited upon by a fez-crowned man carved out of ebony, who dispensed a thin sour wine from a goat-skin, which he carried under his arm like a bagpipe. Not liking the look of the water tank 'midships, I tested this wine early in the voyage, and came to the conclusion that death by thirst was not without its advantages.

The steamer had slipped her moorings and was gliding out of the bay before I noticed the movement, so absorbed had I been in studying the costumes and manners of my fellow-voyagers. What a gayly colored, shabby, picturesque crowd! It was as if some mad masquerade party had burst the bounds of a ball-room and run away to sea. Here was a Tangier merchant in sky-blue gaberdine, with a Persian shawl twisted around his waist, and a black velvet cap set on the back of his head; there a Moor, in snowy turban and fleecy caftan, with a jewel-hilted, crescent-bladed knife at his girdle. Tall slim Arabs, in dingy white robes like those worn by Dominicans, stalked up and down between the heaps of luggage, or leaned over the taffrail in the pitiless sunshine, gazing listlessly into the distance. Others stowed themselves among the freight, and went to sleep. If you seated yourself by chance on what appeared to be a bit of old sail, something stirred

protestingly under you, and a bronze vis-
age slowly unshelled itself from the hood
of a burnoose. Everywhere was some
strange shape. In the bow of the vessel a
fat negro from the Soudan sat cross-legged,
counting his money, which he arranged in
piles on a rug in front of him, the silver on
one side and the copper on the other. He
looked like a Hindoo idol, with his heavy-
lidded orbs and baggy cheeks, the latter
sagging almost down to the folds of flesh
that marked his triple chin, those rings of
the human oak. Near him, but not watching him, and evidently not caring for anything, stood a bareheaded, emaciated old
man. His cranium, as polished and yellow
as ancient ivory, was covered with a delicate tracery of blue veins, and resembled a
geographical globe. At his girdle hung a
leather pouch, apparently containing a few
coins. Both this person and the negro, as
well as the majority of their companions,
were returning from a commercial visit to

Gibraltar. The chief trade of Tangier and the outlying districts consists in supplying the English garrison and the cities of Cadiz and Lisbon with cattle, fowls, fruits, and green stuff. I saw none of these people on the streets of Gibraltar, however. They probably hugged the water-front, where the markets are, and did not venture into the upper town. With their graceful dress they would not have been out of place among the Highland kilts and scarlet coats that light up the *alameda* of a pleasant afternoon.

Already the huge rock of Gibraltar, which is looked upon with such envious and hopeless eyes by the Spaniards, had shrunk to half its proportions. It lay there, gray, grim, and fantastic, like some necromancer's castle on the edge of the sea. Before us was nothing but twinkling sunshine and salt-water. At our right were vague purple peaks and capes, beyond the point of one of which stood the Trafalgar light-house, invisible to us; but who can pass within twenty leagues of it and not think of England's great admiral? The sea was crisped by a refreshing westerly breeze; over us the sky sprung its pale cerulean arch, festooned here and there with shapeless silvery clouds like cobwebs. Fitful odors blown from unseen groves of palm and orange sweetened the air.

> "O happy ship,
> To rise and dip,
> With the blue crystal at your lip!"

The heat of the sun was no longer intolerable. The man at the wheel had thrown back his capote, and was smoking a cigarette. The noisy group of Arabs huddled together round the capstan had ceased their chatter. The fat negro, his pitiful coins counted and laid away, was leaning his head against a coil of rope, and staring with glazed eyeballs at nothing. A hush, a calm, that was not lethargy — for it partook of the nature of a dream — seemed to have fallen upon all.

There were several Europeans aboard besides myself, if I may pass for a European — a Marseillaise gentleman about to join his wife, the guest of her brother, the French consul at Tangier; an Italian gentleman travelling for pleasure (not that the other was not); a Dutch painter from Antwerp, with an amazing porcelain pipe; and last, but not least, a Briton, among whose luggage was a circular tin bath-tub, concerning which the Mohammedan mind had swamped itself in vain conjecture. Was it a piece of defensive armor — a shield, for example — or was it a gigantic frying-pan? These Christian dogs, they have such outlandish fashions! No Arab passed it without a curious glance, and at intervals quite a little crowd would gather about it. Now and then a Jew, who knew what the article was, though he had never used it, smiled superciliously.

We had been under way an hour or more, when I observed the Englishman in deep converse with a personage who had greatly impressed me as I caught a glimpse of him on the gangway at Gibraltar before the boat started. I had lost him a moment afterward, and reluctantly concluded that he had gone ashore again. But there he was, wherever he came from. By the gracious dignity of his manner and the richness of his dress, he might have been Haroun-al-Raschid himself. He was Moorish, but clearly of finer material than the rest. His burnoose, of some soft indigo stuff, was edged with gold, liquid threads of which also ran through the gossamer *caic* bound about his turban. The two ends of this scarf flowed over his shoulders, and crossed themselves on his breast, forming an effective frame for his handsome features. His legs were bare, but the half-slippers covering his feet were of costly make. If he was not a person of consequence, he looked it. I was wondering whether he was a cadi or a pasha, and what he was doing without attendants, when he quitted the

Englishman and went to the water-tank, where the loungers respectfully made room for him. He then performed an act which suggested unutterable things touching that water tank. Instead of helping himself brutally, as the others had done, he gracefully covered his mouth with one of the ends of his caic, and drank through that. I had been drinking this water unfiltered, making an aquarium of myself.

A few minutes later I was surprised to see the man approaching the rear deck, where I occupied a camp-stool, captured and retained after unheard-of struggles. It was plainly his intention to address me. I rose from my seat to receive the card which he held out politely. I here print it in full, for the benefit of future explorers, to whom I heartily commend the Hadji Caddor Sahta,[1] dragoman, king's courier, and gentleman at large:

[1] The title of *Hadji* indicates that the bearer has made the pilgrimage to Mecca.

14

HADJI CADDOR SAHTA.

GUIDE AND INTERPRETER.
Fully conversant with the French, English, Italian, Spanish,
and Arabic languages.
Is likewise disposed to accompany travellers to the interior
of
MOROCCO.
FULLY SECURITY OFFERED.

TANGIER.

The Hadji Caddor — who was better
than his prospectus, for he spoke unexceptionable English — was organizing a party
to visit the ancient city of Fez, and begged
the honor of my company.

"The señor doubtless knows," he said,
"that a caravan leaves for Fez in the
course of a few days. But to travel with
a caravan is to travel with cattle. It is not
so with me; we have our own tents and
slaves and armed escort, and go as gentlemen and princes, thanks be to God and my
personal supervision!"

I explained to the Hadji that my modest
purpose was simply to spend a day in

Africa, and that Tangier was the limit of my desire. Upon this he remarked that his preparations would detain him in the town until the end of the week, and that he laid his services at my feet. I metaphorically picked them up on the spot, and engaged him to show me the sights in Tangier.

While this brief dialogue was passing, an ill-begotten Moor in a dirty turban made off with my camp-stool. He was sitting upon it stolidly a few paces distant. I advanced a step to assert my claims, when the Hadji checked me.

"It is useless," he said, laying one finger softly on the back of my hand. "He's a bad man — Ayoub, the tailor. I know him. Leave him alone. Our Spanish friends have a good proverb, 'It is a waste of lather to shave an ass.' I will get you another seat, señor."

The Hadji Caddor was a philosopher; but, like a great many philosophers, he was philosophical chiefly for other people. If

the case had been his, I am sure he would
not have borne it patiently. After all, one
can not ask more of a stoic than not to cry
out at another man's toothache. The Hadji
was really a character, and if I were painting a figure-piece instead of a landscape; I
would draw him life-size. He had travelled
far and wide, even to the steppes of Tarta-
ry. He spoke several Continental tongues
with singular fluency; Arabic and half a
dozen polyglot dialects were, of course, his
by nature. He was very wise, and, as the
Orientals have it, he had plucked his wis-
dom from the stem of experience. I never
met a more intelligent man, black or white.
His remarks had often a pith of great originality, as when, for instance, in describing
a certain Jew of Algesiras, who had played
him a scurvy trick, he observed, " But he's
nothing, señor, less than nothing — a cipher with the rim removed ! "

We fell to talking on the condition of
Morocco. Was the young Sultan, Muley

el Hassen, popular? Though the Hadji was somewhat guarded in his comments on the imperial government, he gave me a clear idea of the degradation and wretchedness of the people. The territory known as Morocco is inclosed by the Mediterranean, Algeria, the desert of Sahara, and the Atlantic, and is inhabited by a mongrel population of about 800,000 souls. The agriculturists are mostly Arabs and Shelloohs, dwelling on the rich plains; they are poor cultivators, and are taxed to death. The wild Berber tribes, in a chronic state of revolt, occupy the perilous heights and passes of the Atlas chain. The Moors, the Jews, and the blacks crowd themselves into the towns and villages. From the blacks the bulk of the emperor's army is recruited. The Moors, descended principally from the Moors driven out of Spain by Ferdinand and Isabella, are a degenerate race, contaminated by intermarriages with the Arabs. The Jews are precisely what they were in

Europe in the Middle Ages — thrifty, crafty, persecuted, uncomplaining, taking it out of their oppressors in the way of profits; neither their lot nor their nature has been changed by exile. The notable towns are Morocco, the capital, El-Araish, Tafilet, Agadir, Mogadore, Fez, and Tangier. They are all ground into dust under the heel of the emperor. Tangier, the outer breached wall of Islamism, is regarded with particular disfavor, her commerce harassed and her trade strangled by whimsical restrictions. No man there dares own himself rich ; if suspected of secreted wealth, he is tortured until he reveals the hiding-place ; then both his head and his money are removed. The emperor's idea of taxation is the simplest possible : he takes what he wants. There is no appeal. He alters weights, measures, and prices at will ; the multiplication table goes down before him. The sword, the cord, the bastinado, and the branding-iron are ever ready to enforce his

caprice. It is no hyperbole when the court
poet assures this monster that he holds life
and death in the hollow of his hand. He is
the only full-blown despot whose dominions
lie contiguous to civilization. The Czar of
all the Russias is not so much his own master; the Sultan at Constantinople is not so
absolute. The great despot breeds a host
of lesser ones, and it is these that bleed
Morocco unmercifully. The nomadic tribes
have their sheik, the cities their cadi, the
provinces their pasha — and the head devil
at Fez has them all. "But there is no
God but God," said the Hadji Caddor, re-
signedly.

Just then there was a hubbub in the forward part of the ship. Three or four mu-
latto sailors were dragging a slightly built
young man aft, and the slightly built young
man was stoutly resisting. I forgot to state
that shortly after leaving port a person of
insinuating amiability and politeness dis-
tributed himself among the passengers and

collected their tickets. It now appeared
that this person was merely an intoxicated
passenger, with no authority whatever to
act in the matter, and they were dragging
him before the captain. This episode created great merriment. I do not know what
became of the amateur ticket-gatherer —
he was a born humorist, and I trust no
harm befell him — for the cry of " Land ! "
lured me to the bows of the vessel. The
chalky fortress and town of Ceuta — the
Spanish convict station — were fading out
on our left. Presently we rounded Cape
Malabar, and, yes, there was Tangier — an
indistinguishable mass of white that mo-
mentarily shaped itself into crenellated battlements and mosques and huddled house-
tops.

As we dropped anchor within gunshot of
the white-walled town, it lay in the golden
mist of the approaching sunset. Here and
there a projecting piece of snowy stone-
work took a transient rosy tinge, and here

and there a patch of black shadow etched itself against some indentation. At one or two points along the zigzag wall a number of heavy cannon thrust their noses over the parapet, and seemed irresolutely holding their sullen breath as they stared seaward. At the right, the flat-roofed houses stretched like a gigantic marble staircase up the flank of a hill crowned with a citadel (the Kasba, or castle) that commanded the whole of the lower town, the most prominent feature of which was a slender square tower set with richly glazed tiles. These bits of porcelain sparkled like jewels as the lingering sunlight touched them one by one. Behind all this rose a bleak, arid mountain, draped now in delicate violet tints. If Tangier had nothing more to offer than that exquisite view of herself, I should still have been paid for my pilgrimage.

Our anchor had scarcely taken its plunge when a fleet of *barquillos* put out from a strip of beach that fringed the base of the sea-wall, in the shelter of which lay several larger craft drying their canvas after yesterday's rain. I was noting the good effect of the cinnamon-colored lateen-sails against the dazzling white masonry, when the small boats came dashing alongside like pandemonium broken loose. Each of these boats was manned by two or three vociferating, half-naked maniacs, who stood ready to dismember a passenger rather than not get him at all. One could imagine a lot of Algerine pirates about to attack a helpless merchantman. As soon as the quarantine officer gave the signal of permission, the yelling horde clambered up the ship's side and sprang among their victims. It would require a Dantean pen to describe the tumult and confusion that followed. I will only state that I and my impedimenta — which consisted of a hand-bag and an overcoat — went ashore in three boats. That the whole of me went in a single conveyance was owing to the coolness and energy of the Hadji Caddor, who made his way through the crowd to my side by quietly and systematically strangling everybody that opposed him.

As we pushed off from the steamer, the babel of voices rose higher and higher, and above it all I caught the deep ringing intonations of the Englishman — "Come, now, you black rascal, you cawn't be knocking that tub abäut, don't you know!" My Arab captor, a magnificent animal, with the biceps of a gladiator, disdainfully tossed his head, and taking a long oarsweep, remarked, "Aha! Mister Goddam, he have plenty trouble with him dam tub!"

The Hadji smiled gravely on the young barbarian airing his English.

To run a little ahead of my narrative, a Moorish armorer, with three assistants, was summoned to the hotel the next morning to straighten out the Briton's bath-tub, which had been bent almost double, and otherwise banged beyond recognition. The rough boatmen of Malaga and Cadiz are insipid angels compared with those fellows at Tangier.

" A *peseta* for you if you get in first ! " cried the Hadji.

III.

Two other boats reached the landing simultaneously with our own, and a pair of salaming rascals, who appeared to consider me as deeply in their debt as if they had saved my life, approached with my missing personal effects. The Hadji unceremoniously snatched coat and bag from their hands, and led the way up to the city gate, the fellows following on, gesticulating and tearing their hair in despair. We were about to pass under a massive horseshoe archway, when the great cedar-wood doors were suddenly closed on our noses — a stratagem of the guards to wrest a bribe from the unlucky seafarer. The Hadji glanced quickly at the sun, and saw that it yet lacked a few minutes of the lawful hour for closing the gates; then, receiving no response to his summons, he picked up a big fragment of rock, and began to hammer on the iron-clamped portals, accompanying himself with some very vigorous Arabic, which my ignorance of the language did not prevent me from recognizing as oaths of the first magnitude. After considerable hesitation, the bolts were reluctantly drawn, the doors thrown open, and we passed in on the double-quick, taking our way through a dismal walled alley to the hotel. I call it an alley, but it was, in fact, the principal street. It extended from the sea-front to the gate of the Soc-de-Barra, or outside market, and bisected in its course the only public square in Tangier. I learned to know the street very well afterward, for it was the street of the bazars.

The exterior architecture and the interior topography of the hotel to which the Hadji shortly conducted me rather defy description. It was a large rambling building, which somehow included a part of the city

fortifications. You stepped directly from
the cobble-stoned footway into a spacious
chamber, or hall, paved with blood-red tiles
in the Moorish fashion; variegated tiles
and plaques were set in the walls; a lamp
of cut brass hung from the ceiling; in one
corner stood three or four slim-barrelled
Moorish rifles, with stocks curiously carved
and inlaid. There were two doors hung
with bright tapestry, one leading into a
kitchen, and the other into a dining-hall.
The *rez-de-chaussée* was at least compre-
hensible; the rest was mystery. I do not
know now whether the sleeping apartment
assigned me was on the second or the fifth
floor, or if there were any fifth floor. I
mounted a steep staircase, traversed several
corridors, descended a flight of stone steps,
and found myself out-of-doors. Passing
along a rampart originally pierced for cannon, I turned two or three sharp angles,
climbed up some more stone steps, and
stood in a square, whitewashed room. From

the window I had a lovely view of sea and town, and close by the minaret of the Mohammedan mosque lifted itself into the warm evening sky. At a small opening high up in the minaret the muezzin, with outspread arms, was calling the faithful to prayer, and casting the names of Allah and Mohammed to the four points of the compass. I would fain have lingered a while to look on a scene which, realizing some old and half-forgotten dreams of mine, now seemed itself a dream, but the Hadji was waiting outside on the battlements to pilot me down to dinner.

I pass over the tedious ceremony of the *table d'hôte.* I did not go to Tangier to eat ; and perhaps it was well I did not, for neither the favorite national dish called *cúscússú* nor the small coppery oyster that has the assurance to propagate itself on this coast was much to my taste. The guests at table, at the head of which sat the French consul, were all Europeans, and all

in evening dress, except my acquaintance
the Dutch painter, who performed miracles
with some red mullet. After dinner I be-
took myself to the hotel entrance to finish
a cigarette. Several Moors, muffled in
white mantles, and carrying long guns,
lounged in the doorway. Outside, crouched
on the cobble-stones, were three musicians,
with theorbo, mandolin, and triangle, making music like that of the piper of Bujal-
ance, who charged a maravedi for playing,
and ten for leaving off.

The Hadji had planned to take me to an
Arab café — not the café in the square, usually visited by strangers, but an unadul-
terated Arab place of entertainment, seldom profaned by the presence of giaours.
The Antwerp artist and the Englishman
were to accompany us. Just as the edge
of a new moon had begun to cut the dark,
the Hadji appeared with a lantern fastened
to the end of a staff, and we sallied forth.

Save for this lantern and that moon —

15

which did not seem half so good a moon as we have at home — we should have been in Stygian darkness as we stumbled along the unlighted streets. On either hand stretched a high wall, pierced at intervals with a door shaped like a clover leaf, or with a barred casement, divided in the centre by a slender pillar, like the windows in the Alcazar at Seville. There were few persons stirring. Now and then a sheeted figure flitted past us and vanished through an inky archway — possibly some belated slave bearing a scented missive to Fatima or Noureddin. Once we came upon a tall Rifan, with the red cloth case of his gunbarrel twisted round his brows for a turban ; and once the Hadji's lantern lighted up the fierce outlines of a man with a naked scymetar in his hand pursuing some one in the distance. Now and then a fugitive perfume told us we were near a garden, and a stiff palm-tree shot up from behind a wall, and nicked the blue-blackness

of the sky. On we pressed through the
shadows, ourselves shadowy and spectral
and silent. The Hadji, haughty and grave,
with his scabbard clinking along the stones,
seemed like the caliph in the old story-
book, and we his attendants, on some noc-
turnal ramble through the streets of Bag-
dad.

Suddenly our guide halted at a low mean
door. Above it was a dimly lighted lattice,
from which came a murmuring, melancholy
sound of voices, accented by the twanging
of guitar strings. The flame of the lantern
showed us a black hand painted on the
masonry at the left of the entrance. That
hand appears at the door-side of many of
the houses in Tangier, and is a charm to
keep off the evil spirits.

Passing up a flight of well-worn stone
steps, we entered the café — a long narrow
chamber, divided in the centre by the
ever-recurring horseshoe arch. The whitewashed walls were bare of ornament, save

a scarlet vine running round the room just above the mopboard. In the first compartment a negro was making coffee at a shelf suspended from the ceiling. In the other section were the guests, who saluted us with various kinds of stares — curious, insolent, or indifferent, as the mood prompted — after which they ignored our presence as effectively as a group of ill-bred Christians could have done. Sharp-faced Arab youths and full-bearded, vicious-looking old men squatted on the matting. There was not a piece of furniture anywhere, not even one of those dwarf tables frequently to be seen in Moorish houses. From a bronze tripod on which some aloes were burning a bluish thread of smoke lifted itself up spirally, like a rattlesnake ready to spring.

We took our places on the floor like the others, and after a few words from the Hadji, the negro served us with coffee. Each cup was prepared separately, and you were supposed to drink the grounds, which

constituted a third of the allowance. Nevertheless, it was a delicious beverage — up
to the point where it became a solid. Then
four small metal pipes, charged with Turk-
ish tobacco and a grain or two of mild
opium, were brought to us. Meanwhile the
musicians, seated at the upper end of the
room, never ceased their monotonous, whin-
ing strains. Nobody spoke. The younger
fellows lolled back against the wall, motion-
less, with half-shut eyes; the blue smoke
slowly floated up from the pipe-bowls, and
curled itself into arabesque patterns over
the solemn, turbaned heads of the old Mus-
sulmans —

> "Viziers nodding together
> In some Arabian night."

After a while a man of fabulous leanness
arose, and began a kind of dance. He
danced only from the hips upward, sway-
ing his arms in the air as he contorted his
body, and accompanying himself with a
crooning chant. By-and-by his eyes closed

ecstatically, his head leaned far back, an epileptic foam came to his lips. From time to time one of the spectators jerked out a sharp "Jaleo!" to encourage him, others of the audience beat the measure on the palms of their hands, and the tambourines kept up a dull thud. It was in every respect the same dance which the *gitanos* execute less passionately in Granada. The man ended his performance abruptly, and sat down, and all was silent again, except that the doleful, strident music went on and on, with pitiless reiteration of the same notes.

Looking at it carelessly, it struck me that Moorish enjoyment was composed of very simple ingredients; but looking closer, I suspected there were depths and qualities in this profound and nearly austere repose, in this smouldering passion, with its capricious fiery gleams, which I had not penetrated. Perhaps it was the drug in the tobacco, or perhaps it was a pungent property in the coffee, that sharpened my sense, but presently I began to detect in the music, which had rather irritated me at first, an under-current of meaning, vague and perplexing. The slow dragging andante and the sudden wailing falsetto seemed half to assist and half to baffle some inarticulate spirit that strove to distill its secret into the ear. Something that was not the music itself was struggling to find expression through it — the pride, the rage, the inertia, the unutterable despair of an ancient and once mighty people passing away.

IV.

It was Sunday. I do not know whose Sunday it was, for there are three to the week in Tangier, the Mohammedan, the Jew, and the Christian having each his own. It was Sunday; but what was more to the purpose, it was also a market-day. I had caught the town in one of its spasms of business. Between these spasms, and when the Aissawa are not overrunning it, or no fête is going on, the place is said to be as dull and silent as a plague-smitten city.

It being my last as well as my first day in Africa, I did not wait for the Hadji to call me that morning. I was an early bird, astir even before the slightest worm of a breakfast was practicable. Having completed my toilet, I wandered out on the platform in front of my bedroom to kill the

intervening hour. Discovering a stone staircase leading still higher, I mounted the
steps, and found myself on the roof of the
hotel.

The Kasba on the height had all its windows illuminated by the daybreak, but the
rest of the town lay in cool shadow. At
my feet stretched a confused mass of square-
cut white houses, reaching to the sea's edge
on one side, and ending in drifts on the
slant of a hill at my left — a town of snow
that had seemingly dropped flake by flake
from the clouds during the night.

There were figures moving on several of
the neighboring house-tops. All the roofs
were flat, and most of them surrounded by
low battlements. Yonder was a young ne-
gress in a sulphur-hued caftan and green
girdle, shaking a striped rug over a parapet, and looking consciously picturesque.
On a terrace farther off a Moorish washer-
woman and a little girl were spreading out
their härcks and embroidered napkins on

the flag-stones : the sun would reach them
by-and-by. At my right was a man indolently lifting himself off a piece of carpet
laid dangerously near the unprotected roof
edge — possibly a summer boarder who had
chosen that airy bed-chamber. He was rubbing his eyes, and had evidently slept there
over night. In this temperate climate,
where the thermometer seldom rises above
90°, and rarely falls below 40°, the house-
top would be preferable to an inside room
to a summer boarder. On many of the
roofs was evidence of pretty attempts at
gardening, oleanders, acacias, palms, and
dwarf almond-trees being set out in ornamental jars and tubs. There, no doubt, was
the family resort after night-fall, the scene
of ceremonious or social visits, and, I imagine, of much starry love-making.

Behind the hotel, in a desolate vacant
lot checkered by small vats half filled with
dye-stuffs, was an Arab tanner at work.
Standing in the midst of his colored squares

he resembled a solitary chessman. I could look directly down on his smooth bare skull, which seemed cast of gilt-bronze or bell-metal. He wore nothing but a breech-cloth. The Moorish tanners are very expert, and employ arts not known to the trade elsewhere. They have a process by which lion and panther skins are rendered as pliable as satin, and of creamy whiteness. The green leather of Tafilet, the red of Fez, and the yellow of Morocco are highly esteemed.

I was still on the roof-top when the Hadji summoned me to breakfast, immediately after which we set forth on a stroll through the city. The streets of Tangier lose a little on close inspection by daylight; they are very dirty and very narrow, forming a labyrinth from which a stranger could scarcely extricate himself without the grace of God. I was constantly imagining that we had come back to our starting-point, the houses being unnumbered, and without any feature to distinguish one from the other. It was like walking through endless avenues of tombs. Each building presented to the contracted footway an inhospitable, massive wall, set with a door of the exact pattern of its neighbor. This monotony is a characteristic of Oriental street architecture. No wonder the robber chief, in The Forty Thieves, put a chalk-mark on the door of Ali Baba's house in order to find it again ; and no wonder the slave-girl Morgiana completely frustrated the device by marking half a dozen doors in a similar manner.

Whatever of elegance there may be inside the Moorish houses, the outside is careful to give no hint of it. I believe that some of the interiors are lavishly decorated. Once or twice, in passing a half-open gate, I caught sight of a tessellated *patio*, with a fountain set in the midst of flowers and broad-leaved shrubbery, reminding me of the Andalusian court-yards. But the domestic life of the Mussulman goes veiled like his women.

For a city with so many Sundays, Tangier makes a rather poor exhibit in the line of sacred architecture. The foreign legations have a secluded chapel somewhere, and there are several mosques and Jewish synagogues, but none of note, except the Mohammedan mosque, whose porcelain-plated tower is the best part of it. In my quality of Christian dog I was not admitted to the edifice. The Hadji described the interior as being barren of interest. When the faithful go in to devotions they leave their foot-covering in the vestibule. As we went by that morning there were thirty or forty empty slippers of all sizes and colors arranged in a row on the stone pavement. They suggested the remnants of a row of soldiers that had been blown away by some phenomenal volley.

The Moors are handsome men, haughty of feature, and with great dignity of car-

riage. The Arab women, of whom we met
not so many, left their charms to the imagination. Though they were muffled up to
the eyelids, showing only a strip of buff
forehead, they generally turned aside their
faces as we approached them. Their street
costume was not elaborate — a voluminous
linen mantle, apparently covering nothing
but a wide-sleeved chemise reaching to the
instep and caught at the waist. Their bare
feet were thrust into half-slippers, and their
finger-tips stained with henna. Some had
only one eye visible. In the younger women, that one pensive black eye peering
out from the snowy coif was very piquant.
The Hebrew maidens were not so avari-
cious of themselves, but let their beauty
frankly blossom in doorways and at upper
casements. Many of the girls were as slender and graceful as vines. In their apparel
they appeared to affect solid colors — blues,
ochres, carmines, and olive greens. They
have a beautiful national dress, which is

worn only in private. The Jewesses of
Tangier are famous for their eyes, teeth,
and complexions, and for their figures in
early maidenhood. At thirty-five they are
shapeless old women,

" Sans teeth, sans eyes, sans taste, sans — everything."

The increasing number of passers-by, and
a confused buzz of voices that grew every
moment more audible, indicated that we
were nearing some centre of traffic or pleasure. Leaving a fearful alley behind us —
an alley where heaps of refuse were piled
in the middle of the footpath, and the
body of a collapsed cat or dog was continu-
ally blocking the way — we issued upon
the place of the bazars — a narrow winding
hillside thoroughfare, paved with cobble-
stones, and lined on either hand by a series
of small alcoves scooped in the masonry.

In each of these recesses a Jew or an
Arab merchant sat cross-legged upon a little counter, with his goods piled within convenient reach on shelves at his side and

over his head. The counter, which rose to
the height of the customer's breast, was
really the floor of the shop. In one booth
nothing was sold but steel-work — Damascus blades (manufactured round the corner)
with richly wrought hilts; slim Moorish
guns with a profusion of mother-of-pearl
and tortoise-shell inlay on the breeches;
shields, chains, spurs, bits, and the like.
In an angle of the wall, near this booth,
was a half-naked sword-grinder serving a
Bedouin, who leaned on a spear-handle,
and with critical eye watched the progress
of the workman. Here was a tobacconist,
with fragrant Latakia to dispose of, and
snake-stemmed nargilehs in which to burn
it; there, a fruiterer, buried in figs and
dates and sweetmeat confections; farther
on, a jeweller, or a dealer in nicknacks, or
a saddle-maker. The smartest shops were
those of the cloth merchants. At their
doors were displayed rose-colored caftans,
rivulets of scarfs shot with silver thread,

broidered towels, Daghestan rugs, bright
fabrics from Rabatt and Tetuan.

There was no lack of color or animation
in the crowd; no lack of customers beating
their bosoms and exploding with incredu-
lity at the prices demanded (I saw an old
Berber in front of one bazar tear off his
turban and trample on it, to show he would
give no such price); no lack of peripatetic
venders interfering with legitimate trade;
no lack of noisy water-sellers, each with his
sprig of scented shrub laid over his water-
skin; there was, in brief, no lack of anything proper to the scene and the moment;
yet I had a sense of disappointment, and
probably expressed it in my face.

"Then you would be disappointed in the
bazars at Damascus," said the Hadji, sadly,
for he had the honor of Tangier at heart.
"This is Damascus, or any Eastern city, in
small. In the great capitals you would see
more, but nothing different. The bazars at
Constantinople are gay, yes; of European

16

gayety, you understand — only half national.   These are the shops of the people
such as you will see through the East.
But there are other establishments of richer
merchants, to which the wise go.   I will
take you to one.   It is not far."

Before quitting the mart, I entered into
a slight mercantile transaction with the
fruiterer, which resulted in filling both my
pockets to the top with copper coins — the
surprising change due me out of a two-
franc piece.   These coins are worth about a
dollar a bushel.   The five-pointed star, or
Solomon's ring, stamped on one side, is supposed to be a talisman against the evil eye;
but it can scarcely reconcile the Moors to
the fact that the government pays its debts
in this wretched currency, called *flu*, and
will receive nothing for imposts and taxes
but silver or gold.   I was glad, later on, to
deposit that copper with a necromancer in
the Soc-de-Barra, to see what he could do
with it.

The shop of one of the richer merchants to which the wise go, and where the Hadji incontinently took me, was located on the second floor of a private house in an adjacent side street. As it was the sole house that was likely to show me its penetralia, I noted that it had a square court in the centre open to the sky, and that all the apartments in the second story gave upon a gallery overlooking this court-yard. Here were three large rooms packed from floor to cornice with a little of everything on earth — arms, jewelry, costumes, bronzes, Moorish faience, sandal-wood boxes, amber beads, old brass lamps (for which any Aladdin would have been glad to exchange new ones), and bale upon bale of silks and fairy textures from looms of Samarcand and Bokhara. Here, also, was a merchant who pulled a face as smooth as a mirror while he demanded four times the value of his merchandise. Nevertheless, I purchased, on reasonable enough terms, a chiselled

brass cresset and an ancient Moorish scent-
bottle in silver. But the possession of these
did not console me for all the tantalizing
drapery and golden bric-à-brac I was unable to purchase.

"Not to desire or admire, if a man could learn it, were more
Than to walk all day like the Sultan of old in a garden of
spice."

The truly wise wouldn't go to the shop of
Selam-Ben-Rhaman!

Passing out into the open air again, we
threaded several tortuous lanes, which
clearly had not been visited by a scaven-
ger's cart within the present century, and
struck the main street at a point near the
double gates leading to the Soc-de-Barra.
Speaking of carts, there is not one of any
description in Tangier. If the pedestrian
gets himself run over there, it must be by
a donkey pure and simple.

A dozen steps brought us outside the
turreted wall of the town to the foot of the
hill called Soc-de-Barra, upon a slope of

which was the market-place — a barren
stretch of sun-scorched earth, broken here
and there by dunes of reddish-gray sand.
In the middle foreground was the caved-in
mausoleum of some forgotten saint, and on
the ridge of the slope an old cemetery, so
dreary with its few hopeless fig-trees and
aloes that it made the heart ache to look at
it. Nothing ever gave me such a poignant
sense of death and dusty oblivion as those
crumbling tombs overshadowing the clam-
orous and turbulent life on the hill-side.

At first the spectacle was bewildering,
and it was only by concentrating my attention on detached groups and figures that I
was able to form any distinct impression of
it. One's eyes were dazzled by the innumerable purple caftans and red fezes and
snowy turbans, mingling and separating,
and melting every instant into some grotesque and harmonious combination, like
the bits of colored glass in a kaleidoscope.
The usual hurly-burly of a market-day had

been added to by the unexpected arrival of
a caravan from Fez.

The unloading of the packs was now going on amid the incessant angry disputes of
the Arab porters and occasional remonstra-
tive groans from the gaunt camels kneeling
in the hot sand. Near by, on a lean horse,
sat a Bedouin, with his gun slung over the
pommel. He was dirty and ragged, but
his crimson saddle-cloth was worked with
gold braid, and metal ornaments dangled
from his bridle. Bending a trifle forward
in the saddle, the son of the desert seemed
to be intently observing the porters, but in
reality he was half listening to an elderly
Arab who sat on the ground a few paces
distant, surrounded by a wholly absorbed
circle of listeners. It was curious to watch
their mobile faces reflecting, like so many
mirrors, the various changes in the expression of the speaker. He was telling a story
— a story that required much pressing of
the hand against the heart and many swift

transitions from joy to despair, and finally
involved a pantomime of a person on horseback carrying off somebody. A love-story!
Perhaps one of Scheherezade's. The spirit,
though not the letter, of it reached me. I
noticed, with proper professional pride, that
neither the mountebank near the saint's
tomb, nor the snake-charmer farther up the
slope, had so large an audience as the story-
teller.

The snake-tamer, however, honestly
earned his hire by letting an ugly cobra de
capello draw blood from his cheek to the
slow music of a reed pipe and a tambourine
played by a couple of assistants. After
wondering at the man, I began to wonder
at the serpent for biting so hideous an object. Only less hideous was his neighbor,
the necromancer, who did some really
clever feats of fire-eating, and became the
recipient at my hands of about two pounds
of copper *flu.* The gratuity seemed to have
the effect of putting an end to his perform-

ance, for he abruptly disappeared after this accession of wealth.

Both these men, as well as the several mendacious "saints" who were collecting tribute of the crowd, belonged to that fanatical sect known as the Aissawa, whose periodic incursions in force into Tangier must be more picturesque than agreeable, if the Hadji gave me a true account of them. His description did not materially differ from that which I find in an admirable work on Morocco by Edmondo de Amicis, from which I quote: "The Aissawa are one of the principal religious confraternities of Morocco, founded, like the others, under the inspiration of God, by a saint called Sidi-Mohammed-ben-Aissa, born at Mekïnez two centuries ago. . . . They have a great mosque at Fez, which is the central house of the order, and from thence they spread themselves every year over the provinces of the empire, gathering together as they go those members of the brotherhood who are in towns and villages. Their rites, similar to those of the howling and whirling dervishes of the East, consist in a species of frantic dances, interspersed with leaps, yells, and contortions, in the practice of which they grow ever more furious and ferocious, until, losing the light of reason, they crush wood and iron with their teeth, burn their flesh with glowing coals, wound themselves with knives, swallow mud and stones, brain animals and devour them alive and dripping with blood, and finally fall to the ground insensible."

If I had chosen my day in Africa a week earlier, I should have witnessed one of those edifying festivals; but I missed that, as well as the fête of the birth of Mohammed, on which occasion the Soc-de-Barra is a very gay spot. At all times, I fancy, it is little more than a barbaric play-ground.

So far as I could observe, its special claims as a market were sustained this day only by four or five isolated clusters of aged crones, who squatted under striped awnings, and sold bread, pottery, and a kind of grain called *durra*, which forms the staple food of the lower classes. I have seen few specimens of Tangier pottery in collections. It is very rude, and utterly wanting in most of the qualities usually prized; but its brilliant glaze and the barbaric fancy of some of its designs entitle it to consideration. I am speaking of the ware used by the common people. The only lively trade I saw carried on in the market was done in those gaudily tinted jars and vases.

The majority of the crowd seemed to have no purpose whatever beyond wandering from point to point and indulging in as many gesticulations as possible. Now and then a mysterious hush fell upon the throng, a breathless silence broken an instant afterward by universal chatter. Neither the sudden silence nor the sudden clamor explained itself. Underlying it all was a profound melancholy. Here, three or four half-grown Soudan negroes lay on their backs, blinking at the sky; there, a squad of venerable Rifans leaned apathetically against a whitewashed wall in the strong sunshine — meagre, dry old men, looking like mummies, that had warmed into a semblance of life, and had partially thrown aside their cerements. The moment a person ceased speaking and moving, he became a statue of weariness. It was a relief to watch a score or two of comical little Arab boys — the exact pattern of Tanagra *figurines* — darting in and out among the confusion of legs, and making up impertinent faces under their peaked hoods, as some irate by-stander from time to time gave one of them an impromptu taste of a lance-handle.

Suddenly I caught a glimpse of my fellow-voyager the Dutch artist, with his easel planted in a shadow of the wrinkled wall, sketching away like mad. I envied him, for to a painter this Soc-de-Barra should be a mine of wealth. Indeed, all Tangier is that. Fortuny and Henri Regnault have taught us how rich it is. The latter, after receiving the Prix de Rome, resided a long time in Tangier. It was here he painted his magnificent " Exécution sans Jugement sous les Rois maures de Grenade "; and it was from his Arabian dreams in the old Moorish town that he awoke at the fall of Sedan, and hurried to give his life, as freely as he had given his genius, to France. Regnault met his death, futilely, in almost the last engagement of the war — if it is futile to be a hero.

He was still in my thought as I turned back to the city gate, for my next excursion was to the hill of the Kasba — a spot associated with his memory. The treasury building in the Kasba furnished him with the background of his " Sortie du Pacha " — one of Regnault's masterpieces.

Without this fact the citadel itself would poorly have rewarded me for the hot climb up the hill-side. The governor, or bashaw, has his residence in the castle, which is garrisoned. I believe there was a horrible prison hidden somewhere in its depths, but I did not attempt to visit it. Doubtless the stucco-work of the innumerable apartments I looked into was once as gorgeous with gold-leaf and pigment as the mezquita at Cordova, or the Hall of the Abencerrages in the Alhambra; but nothing of the past richness remained. Here and there on a moulding or at the base of a column a line in Cufic characters or an embossed sentence from the Koran tamely wriggled out from the whitewash. That was all. The sacrilegious brush of man had done as much damage there as the hand of time.

The architecture did not pay me for my pains, but I was amply paid by being allowed to assist at a Moorish court of justice, upon which the Hadji and I stumbled by chance. The judge, or cadi — I am not positive as to the cadiship — was seated on a Persian rug in the middle of a room small enough and gloomy enough to be a cell. Behind him was ranged a row of barefooted soldiers; in front of him stood plaintiff and defendant, alike abject. Each in turn delivered himself of a long speech containing frequent allusions to Allah, and relapsed into silence. When the pair had finished, the flabby judge sat awhile, ruminative, with his chin buried in his beard; then he lifted his face and pronounced sentence. Without more ado, one of the men — the plaintiff, likely enough — was hauled into the court-yard, just outside, and preparations were making to give him a dozen lashes with a cat-o'-nine-tails, when we hastened our departure. I expected nothing but to see his head snipped off before we could get out of the place. A vision of that splash of blood on the white marble stairs in Regnault's picture danced in front of my eyes.

The Hadji laughingly remarked that the

fellow had met with no more than his de-
serts. The laws of Morocco are extremely
severe ; it is seldom that either the guilty
or the innocent escape. The penalty for
petty larceny is so rigorous that the offense
is comparatively unknown, except in the
interior, where robbery and murder are recognized professions. The nomads and the
people of the *duars* live by plundering car-
avans and straggling travellers. But at
Tangier, under the flags of the legations, a
stranger's life and property are more secure
than in one of our American cities. In a
community where a man loses his right
hand if he helps himself to somebody else's
hen, the love of poultry, for example, becomes discreet and chastened. The door of
my bedroom at the hotel had no fastening
on it, and needed none.

It was now three o'clock, and time for
me to return to the inn. My twenty-four
hours of Africa were drawing to a close.
The little steamer that was to take me

back to Gibraltar, immediately after an
early dinner, was already spreading some
coquettish sooty curls over her smoke-stack.
Before descending to level ground, and
plunging once more into the intricacies of
the lower town, I lingered a few minutes
on the heights of the Kasba to take a fare-
well look.

It is a very ancient city, the oldest city
but one in the world. The Moors of Spain
in the time of Aboo-Abdallah made pilgrimages to it on account of its antiquity. The
cloth-merchants, and the swarthy money-
changers, and the shrill water-carriers were
plying their trade, and all the indolent, feverish life we witness to-day was seething,
in these narrow streets when Christ was a
little child in Nazareth.

Founded in some unknown period, by
the Carthaginians it is supposed, Tangier
— the Tingis of the Romans — has always
been a bone of bloody contention among

IX.

ON GETTING BACK AGAIN.

IX.

ON GETTING BACK AGAIN.

THIS page will be wafted possibly through a snow-storm to the reader's hand; but it is written while a few red leaves are still clinging to the maple bough, and the last steamer of the year from across the ocean has not yet discharged on our shores the final cargo of returning summer tourists. How glad they will be, like those who came over in previous ships, to sight that phantomish, white strip of Yankee land called Sandy Hook! It is thinking of them that I write.

Some one — that anonymous person who is always saying the wisest and most delightful things just as you are on the point of saying them yourself — has remarked that one of the greatest pleasures of foreign

travel is to get home again. But no one —
that irresponsible person forever to blame
in railway accidents, but whom, on the
whole, I vastly prefer to his garrulous rela-
tive quoted above — no one, I repeat, has
pointed out the composite nature of this
pleasure, or named the ingredient in it
which gives the chief charm to this getting
back. It is pleasant to feel the pressure of
friendly hands once more; it is pleasant to
pick up the threads of occupation which
you dropped abruptly, or perhaps neatly
knotted together and carefully laid away,
just before you stepped on board the steamer; it is very pleasant, when the summer
experience has been softened and subli-
mated by time, to sit of a winter night by
the cheery wood fire, or even at the regis-
ter, since one must make one's self comfortable in so humiliating a fashion, and let
your fancy wander back in the old foot-
prints; to form your thoughts into happy
summer pilgrims, and dispatch them to

Arles or Nuremberg, or up the vine-clad heights of Monte Cassino, or embark them at Vienna for a cruise down the swift Danube to Buba-Pesth. But in none of these things lies the subtile charm I wish to indicate. It lies in the refreshing, short-lived pleasure of being able to look at your own land with the eyes of an alien; to see novelty blossoming on the most commonplace and familiar stems; to have the old manner and the threadbare old custom present themselves to you as absolutely new — or if not new, at least strange. After you have escaped from the claws of the custom-house officers — who are not nearly as affable birds as you once thought them — and are rattling in an oddly familiar hack through well-known but half-unrecognizable streets, you are struck by something comical in the names on the shop signs, — *are* American names comical, as Englishmen seem to think? — by the strange fashion of the iron lamp-post at the corner, by peculiarities in the architecture, which you ought to have noticed, but never did notice until now. The candid incivility of the coachman, who does not touch his hat to you, but swears at you, has the vague charm of reminiscence. You regard him as the guests regarded the poor relation at table, in Lamb's essay; you have an impression that you have seen him somewhere before. The truth is, for the first time in your existence, you have a full, unprejudiced look at the shell of the civilization from which you emerged when you went abroad. Is it a pretty shell? Is it a satisfactory shell? Not entirely. It has strange excrescences and blotches on it. But it is a shell worth examining; it is the best *you* can ever have; and it is expedient to study it very carefully the two or three weeks immediately following your return to it, for your privilege of doing so is of the briefest tenure. Some precious things you do not lose, but your newly acquired vision fails you shortly. Suddenly, while you are comparing, valuing, and criticising, the old scales fall over your eyes, you insensibly slip back into the well-worn grooves, and behold all outward and most inward things in nearly the same light as your untravelled neighbor, who has never known

> " The glory that was Greece
> And the grandeur that was Rome."

You will have to go abroad again to renew those magical spectacles which enabled you for a few weeks to see your native land.

Works of Fiction

PUBLISHED BY

HOUGHTON, MIFFLIN AND COMPANY,

4 PARK STREET, BOSTON, MASS.

Thomas Bailey Aldrich.

Story of a Bad Boy. Illustrated. 12mo	$1.50
Marjorie Daw and Other People. 12mo	1.50
Prudence Palfrey. 12mo	1.50
The Queen of Sheba. 12mo	1.50
The Stillwater Tragedy. 12mo	1.50

Hans Christian Andersen.

Complete Works. First complete edition in English, published by arrangement with the author. The set complete in ten uniform volumes, crown 8vo.

1. The Improvisatore ; or, Life in Italy	1.50
2. The Two Baronesses	1.50
3. O. T. ; or, Life in Denmark	1.50
4. Only a Fiddler	1.50
5. In Spain and Portugal	1.50
6. A Poet's Bazaar	1.50
7. Pictures of Travel	1.50
8. The Story of my Life. With portrait	1.50
9. Wonder Stories told for Children. Ninety-two illustrations.	1.50
10. Stories and Tales. Illustrated.	1.50
The set, cloth	15.00
Half calf	32.50

William Henry Bishop.

Detmold : A Romance. "Little Classic" style. 18mo	1.25
The House of a Merchant Prince. 12 mo.	1.50

Björnstjerne Björnson.

Works. An American edition, sanctioned by the author, and translated by Professor R. B. Anderson, of the University of Wisconsin. In seven volumes, 16mo.

Synnöve Solbakken $1.00
Arne 1.00
A Happy Boy 1.00
The Fisher Maiden 1.00
The Bridal March, and other Stories. 1.00
Captain Mansana, and other Stories 1.00
Magnhild 1.00

Mary Clemmer.

His Two Wives. 12mo 1.50

James Fenimore Cooper.

Complete Works. *Household Edition.* With Introductions to many of the volumes by Susan Fenimore Cooper, and illustrations. In thirty-two volumes, 16mo.

Precaution.	The Prairie.
The Spy.	Wept of Wish-ton-Wish.
The Pioneers.	The Water Witch.
The Pilot.	The Bravo.
Lionel Lincoln.	The Heidenmauer.
Last of the Mohicans	The Headsman.
Red Rover.	The Monikins.
Homeward Bound.	Miles Wallingford.
Home as Found.	The Red Skins.
The Pathfinder.	The Chainbearer.
Mercedes of Castile.	Satanstoe.
The Deerslayer.	The Crater.
The Two Admirals.	Jack Tier.
Wing and Wing.	The Sea Lions.
Wyandotté.	Oak Openings.
Afloat and Ashore.	The Ways of the Hour.

Each volume sold separately.

Cloth, per volume 1.00
Cloth, the set 32.00
Half calf, the set 80.00
Works. *Globe Edition.* With thirty-two original illustrations, by Darley, Dielman, Fredericks, Sheppard, and Waud. In sixteen volumes, 12mo 20.00
Half calf 43.00

(Sold only in sets.)

Sea Tales. *Household Edition.* Illustrated. Ten volumes, 16mo, comprising,

The Pilot.	The Sea Lions.
The Red Rover.	The Water Witch.
Jack Tier.	Afloat and Ashore.
The Two Admirals.	Miles Wallingford.
Wing and Wing.	The Crater.

    Cloth, black and gold $10.00
    Half calf 25.00

Leather-Stocking Tales. *Household Edition.* Illustrated. Five volumes, cloth, black and gold . . . 5.00
    Half calf 12.50

The same. *Riverside Edition.* With valuable Introductions by Susan Fenimore Cooper, numerous illustrations, and a steel portrait of Cooper. Five volumes comprising,

The Deerslayer.	The Pioneers.
The Pathfinder.	The Prairie.
Last of the Mohicans.	

    Cloth, black and gold 11.25
    Half calf 20.00

Cooper Stories; being Narratives of Adventure selected from his Works. With illustrations by F. O. C. Darley.

Stories of the Prarie.	Stories of the Woods.
Stories of the Sea.	

    Per volume, 16mo 1.00
    The set, 3 vols 3.00

Maria S. Cummins.

The Lamplighter. 12mo 1.50
El Fureidîs. 12mo 1.50
Mabel Vaughan. *New Edition.* 12mo 1.50

Daniel De Foe.

Robinson Crusoe. Eight illustrations by Thomas Nast, and others by E. Bayard. 16mo 1.00

P. Deming.

Adirondack Stories. "Little Classic" style. 18mo . .75

Thomas DeQuincey.

Romances and Extravaganzas. *Riverside Edition.*
    Crown 8vo 1.50
Narrative and Miscellaneous Papers. *Riverside Edition.* Crown 8vo 1.50

Charles Dickens.

Complete Works. *Illustrated Library Edition.* With Introductions, biographical and historical, by E. P. Whipple. Containing all the illustrations that have appeared in the English edition by Cruikshank, Phiz, Seymour, John Leech, Maclise, Marcus Stone, and others, engraved on steel, to which are added the designs of F. O. C. Darley and John Gilbert, in all numbering over 550. Handsomely bound, and complete in twenty-nine volumes, crown 8vo, as follows : —

The Pickwick Papers, 2 vols.
Nicholas Nickleby, 2 vols.
Oliver Twist.
Old Curiosity Shop, and Reprinted Pieces, 2 vols.
Barnaby Rudge, and Hard Times, 2 vols.
Martin Chuzzlewit, 2 vols.
Our Mutual Friend, 2 vols.
Uncommercial Traveller.
A Child's History of England, and Other Pieces.
Christmas Books.

Dombey and Son, 2 vols.
Pictures from Italy, and American Notes.
Bleak House, 2 vols.
Little Dorrit, 2 vols.
David Copperfield, 2 vols.
A Tale of Two Cities.
Great Expectations.
Edwin Drood, Master Humphrey's Clock, and Other Pieces.
Sketches by Boz.

Cloth, each $1.50
The set in cloth. With Dickens Dictionary.
30 vols 45.00
The set, half calf 100.00

Works. *Globe Edition.* Printed in large type (long primer) on good paper, and containing all the illustrations of Darley and Gilbert (55 in number) on steel, and the Index of Characters. In fifteen volumes, 12mo.

Cloth, per volume 1.25
The set 18.75
The set, half calf, or half morocco 40.00
The set, half russia 45.00

Christmas Carol. Illustrated. 8vo 3.00
Morocco 7.50
Christmas Books. Illustrated. Crown 8vo 2.00
Morocco 5.00

Edgar Fawcett.

A Hopeless Case. "Little Classic" style. 18mo . . 1.25
A Gentleman of Leisure. "Little Classic" style. 18mo 1.00

Fénelon.

Adventures of Telemachus. Crown 8vo 2.25

Baron de la Motte Fouqué.

Undine.
Sintram.
These two, with St. Pierre's "Paul and Virginia,"
32mo $0.75
Undine and other Tales. Illustrated. "Riverside
Classics." 16mo 1.00

Johann Wolfgang von Goethe.

Wilhelm Meister. Translated by Thomas Carlyle.
Portrait of Goethe. 2 vols., 12mo 3.00
The Tale and Favorite Poems. 32mo 75

Oliver Goldsmith.

Vicar of Wakefield. "Little Classic" style. 18mo . 1.00
The same. "Riverside Classics." Illustrated. 16mo 1.00

Jeanie T. Gould.

Marjorie's Quest. Illustrated. 12mo 1.50

Thomas Chandler Haliburton.

The Clockmaker ; or, The Sayings and Doings of
Samuel Slick of Slickville. "Riverside Classics."
Illustrated by Darley. 16mo 1.00

A. S. Hardy.

But yet a Woman. 16mo 1.25

Bret Harte.

The Luck of Roaring Camp and other Sketches. 16mo 1.50
Condensed Novels. Illustrated. 16mo 1.50
Mrs. Skaggs's Husbands, and other Sketches. 16mo 1.50
Tales of the Argonauts, and other Stories. 16mo . . 1.50
Thankful Blossom. A Revolutionary Romance of
the Jerseys. "Little Classic" style. 18mo . . . 1.25
Two Men of Sandy Bar. A Play. "Little Classic"
style. 18mo 1.00
The Story of a Mine. "Little Classic" style. 18mo 1.00
Drift from Two Shores. "Little Classic" style. 18mo 1.25
The Twins of Table Mountain, and other Sketches.
"Little Classic" style. 18mo 1.25
Flip ; and Found at Blazing Star. "Little Classic"
style. 18mo 1.00
Works. Rearranged, with an Introduction and a
Portrait. In five volumes, crown 8vo.

The contents of the different volumes are as follows : —
Vol. I. Poetical Works, and the drama, "Two Men of
        Sandy Bar," with an Introduction by the author,
        and a steel portrait.
Vol. II. "The Luck of Roaring Camp," and other Stories.
Vol. III. Tales of the Argonauts and Eastern Sketches.
Vol. IV. "Gabriel Conroy."
Vol. V. Stories and "Condensed Novels."
    Price per volume $2.00
    The set, half calf 20.00

Julian Hawthorne.

Idolatry. A Romance. 12mo 2.00

Nathaniel Hawthorne.

Works. "Little Classic" Edition. Each volume contains
  a new Vignette Illustration.
Twice-Told Tales. 2 vols.
The Snow-Image, and other Twice-Told Tales.
Mosses from an Old Manse. 2 vols.
The Scarlet Letter.
The House of the Seven Gables.
The Blithedale Romance.
The Marble Faun. A Romance of Monte Beni. 2 vols.
Our Old Home. A Series of English Sketches.
True Stories from History and Biography.
The Wonder-Book for Girls and Boys.
Tanglewood Tales.
American Note-Books. 2 vols.
English Note-Books. 2 vols.
French and Italian Note-Books. 2 vols.
Septimius Felton ; or, The Elixir of Life.
Fanshawe, and other Pieces.
The Dolliver Romance, and other Pieces.
Hawthorne Index.
    In 24 volumes. 18mo, each 1.25
    The set, cloth, in box 30.00
    The set, half calf, or half morocco 60.00
    The set, tree calf 78.00
Works. *Illustrated Library Edition.* In 13 vols. 12mo.
  Each volume has two fine illustrations. Price per vol. 2.00
    The set, cloth 25.00
    The set, half calf 50.00
Works. Volumes of the original 16mo edition still in
  stock : —
Twice-Told Tales. Steel portrait. 2 vols. 3.00
The Snow-Image 1.50

The Scarlet Letter $1.50
The Marble Faun.   2 vols. 3.00
Septimius Felton 1.50
Works.   *Fireside Edition.* With 23 Vignette Illustrations.
  Complete in 13 volumes, including the Index volume.
  16mo.
      The set 21.00
      Half calf 42.00
      Tree calf 53.00
              (*Sold only in sets.*)
The Scarlet Letter. *Holiday Edition.* Beautifully illus-
  trated by Mary Hallock Foote. Red-line border . 4.00
      Morocco, or tree calf 9.00
Tales of the White Hills.
Legends of New England.
      These two, with Fields's Essay on Hawthorne. 32mo   .75
Legends of Province House.
A Virtuoso's Collection.
      These two, with Carlyle's Oliver Cromwell, 32mo .   .75
Works.   *New Globe Edition.*   Complete in 6 vols.
  16mo. With 24 illustrations. The set 10.00
      Half calf 20.00
              (*Sold only in sets.*)
Works.   *New Riverside Edition.* With an original etching
  in each volume, and a new portrait. With bibliographical
  notes by George P. Lathrop. Complete in twelve volumes,
  crown 8vo. Price per vol. 2.00
Hawthorne Index. An Analytical Index to the Works
  of Nathaniel Hawthorne, with a Sketch of his Life.
  Uniform with the "Little Classic" Edition of Hawthorne's Works 1.25
Also uniform with the *Library Edition* 2.00
Uniform with *Fireside Edition* 1.75

Oliver Wendell Holmes.

Elsie Venner. A Romance of Destiny. 12mo . . 2.00
The Guardian Angel. 12mo 2.00

Blanche Willis Howard.

One Summer. A Novel. "Little Classic" style
  18mo 1.25
The same. *Holiday Edition.* Illustrated by Hoppin.
  8vo 2.50

William Dean Howells.

Their Wedding Journey. Illustrated. 12mo . . . 1.50
The same. Illustrated. Paper. 16mo 50
The same. "Little Classic" style. 18mo 1.25

A Chance Aquaintance. Illustrated. 12mo $1.50
The same. Illustrated. Paper. 16mo 50
The same. " Little Classic " style. 18mo 1.25
A Foregone Conclusion. 12mo 1.50
The Lady of the Aroostook. 12mo 1.50
The Undiscovered Country. 12mo 1.50

Thomas Hughes.

Tom Brown's School-Days at Rugby. *New Illustrated
  Edition.* 16mo 1.00
Tom Brown at Oxford. In one volume. 16mo . . . 1.25

Henry James, Jr.

Passionate Pilgrim, and other Tales. 12mo 2.00
Roderick Hudson. *New and Revised Edition.* 12mo 2.00
The American. 12mo 2.00
Watch and Ward. " Little Classic " style. 18mo . 1.25
The Europeans. 12mo 1.50
Confidence. 12mo. 1.50
The Portrait of a Lady. 12mo 2.00

Anna Jameson,

Studies and Stories. " Little Classic " style. 18mo . 1.50

Douglas Jerrold.

Mrs. Caudle's Curtain Lectures. " Riverside Classics."
  Illustrated. 16mo 1.00

Sarah Orne Jewett.

Deephaven. " Little Classic " style. 18mo 1.25
Old Friends and New. " Little Classic " style. 18mo 1.25
Country By-Ways. 18mo 1.25

Rossiter Johnson.

Little Classics.

I. Exile.	X. Childhood.
II. Intellect.	XI. Heroism.
III. Tragedy.	XII. Fortune.
IV. Life.	XIII. Narrative Poems.
V. Laughter.	XIV. Lyrical Poems.
VI. Love.	XV. Minor Poems.
VII. Romance.	XVI. Nature.
VIII. Mystery.	XVII. Humanity.
IX. Comedy.	XVIII. Authors.

Each in one volume. 18mo $1.00
The set, in box, cloth 18.00
The set, in box, half calf, or half morocco . . . 45.00
The same. In 9 vols., square 16mo. The set . . . 13.50
Half calf 27.00
Tree calf 40.50
(*Sold only in sets*)

Charles and Mary Lamb.

Tales from Shakespeare. 18mo 1.00
The same. Illustrated. 16mo 1.00

George Parsons Lathrop.

An Echo of Passion. 16mo 1.25

Henry Wadsworth Longfellow.

Hyperion. A Romance. 16mo 1.50
The same. *Popular Edition.* Cloth, 16mo 40
The same. *Popular Edition.* Paper, 16mo 15
Outre-Mer. 16mo 1.50
The same. *Popular Edition.* Cloth, 16mo 40
The same. *Popular Edition.* Paper, 16mo 15
Kavanagh. 16mo 1.50

Nora Perry.

The Tragedy of the Unexpected and other Stories.
"Little Classic" style. 18mo 1.25

Elizabeth Stuart Phelps.

The Gates Ajar. 16mo 1.50
Men, Women, and Ghosts. 16mo 1.50
Hedged In. 16mo 1.50
The Silent Partner. 16mo 1.50
The Story of Avis. 16mo 1.50
Sealed Orders, and other Stories. 16mo 1.50
Friends : A Duet. 16mo 1.25
Doctor Zay. 16mo 1.25

Joseph Xavier Boniface Saintine.

Picciola. "Riverside Classics." Illustrated. 16mo . 1.00

Jacques Henri Bernardin de Saint-Pierre.

Paul and Virginia. "Riverside Classics." Illustrated
by Hoppin. 16mo 1.00
The same, together with Undine, and Sintram. 32mo . .75

Sir Walter Scott.

Works. The Waverley Novels. *Illustrated Library Edition.*
This edition has been carefully edited and is illustrated
with 100 engravings by Darley, Dielman, Fredericks, Low,
Share, Sheppard, and other artists.   The introduction
which appeared in the Abbotsford Edition, and the illustrated notes inserted in subsequent editions, have been re-
produced here, furnishing all needed explanation of the
novels and the history of their production.   There are also
a glossary and a very full index of characters.   In 25 volumes, crown 8vo, as follows : —

Waverley.	The Fortunes of Nigel.
Guy Mannering.	Peveril of the Peak.
The Antiquary.	Quentin Durward.
Rob Roy.	St. Ronan's Well.
Old Mortality.	Redgauntlet.
Black Dwarf and Legend	The Betrothed, and the High-
of Montrose.	land Widow.
Heart of Mid-Lothian.	The Talisman and other Tales.
Bride of Lammermoor.	Woodstock.
Ivanhoe.	The Fair Maid of Perth.
The Monastery.	Anne of Geierstein.
The Abbot.	Count Robert of Paris.
Kenilworth.	The Surgeon's Daughter, and
The Pirate.	Castle Dangerous.

Price per volume, cloth $1.00
The set, in cloth 25.00
The set, half calf 62.50

The same. *Globe Edition.* Complete in 13 volumes.
12mo, with 100 Illustrations 16.25
Half calf 35.00
(Sold only in sets.)

Tales of a Grandfather. With six steel plates. *Illus-
trated Library Edition.* 3 volumes, crown 8vo, cloth 4.50
Half calf 9.00
Ivanhoe. Fancy binding. 16mo 1.00

Horace E. Scudder.

The Dwellers in Five-Sisters' Court. 16mo, cloth,
black and gold 1.25
Stories and Romances. 16mo 1.25

Mark Sibley Severance.

Hammersmith : His Harvard Days. *New Edition.*
12mo 1.50

J. E. Smith.

Oakridge : An Old-Time Story of Maine   12mo . . $2.00

Mary A. Sprague.

An Earnest Trifler. 16mo 1.25

Harriet Beecher Stowe.

Agnes of Sorrento. 12mo 1.50
The Pearl of Orr's Island. 12mo 1.50
Uncle Tom's Cabin.   *Popular Illustrated Edition*
12mo 2.00
The Minister's Wooing. 12mo 1.50
The Mayflower, and other Sketches. 12mo . . . 1.50
Nina Gordon (formerly called " Dred "). 12mo . . 1.50
Oldtown Folks. 12mo 1.50
Sam Lawson's Fireside Stories. Illustrated. *New*
and enlarged Edition 1.50
The above eight volumes in box 12.00
Uncle Tom's Cabin. *Illustrated Edition.* An entirely new
edition, from new plates, printed with red line border.
With an Introduction, and a Bibliography of the various
editions and languages in which the work has appeared,
by Mr. George Bullen, of the British Museum. Over 100
Illustrations. 12mo 3.50
Half calf 6.50
Morocco, or tree calf 8.00
The same. *Illustrated Subscription Edition.* With
106 Illustrations. 8vo.
(*Sold only by Subscription.*)

Julian Sturgis.

Dick's Wandering. 16mo 1.50

Adeline D. T. Whitney.

Faith Gartney's Girlhood. 12mo 1.50
Hitherto : A Story of Yesterdays. 12mo 1.50
Patience Strong's Outings. 12mo 1.50
The Gayworthys. 12mo 1.50
Leslie Goldthwaite. Illustrated. 12mo 1.50
We Girls : A Home Story. Illustrated. 12mo . . . 1.50
Real Folks. Illustrated. 12mo 1.50
The Other Girls. Illustrated. 12mo 1.50
Sights and Insights. 2 vols. 12mo 3.00

Odd, or Even ?   12mo $1.50

Boys at Chequasset.   12mo 1.50

The above 12 volumes in box 18.00

Gen. Lew Wallace.

The Fair God ; or, The Last of the 'Tzins.   A Tale
of the Conquest of Mexico.   12mo . . : . . . 1.50

⁎ *For sale by all Booksellers.   Sent, post-paid, on receipt of price (in
check on Boston or New York, money-order, or registered letter) by the
Publishers,*

HOUGHTON, MIFFLIN AND COMPANY.

4 Park St., Boston, Mass.; 11 East Seventeenth St.,
New York.

*A Catalogue containing portraits of many of the above authors,
with a description of their works, will be sent free, on application,
to any address.*